# Just

# A

# Forgotten

# Hero

*He survived the war, but it still cost him his life.*

## by

## Rob Moffitt

CW01497757

# Contents

# Preamble

## Introduction

The following is an entirely true tale, and tells the story of a search for living descendants of an ex-RAF Air Gunner who was shot down over Belgium during World War 2. The time-line of the search is accurate, and told from my point of view as one of those concerned in that quest.

Many aspects of the fascinating and involving story of this airman's life and experiences were uncovered during the research and these are included in this tale. How could they not be? While many of these are unique and specific to this one man, many other forgotten heroes shared the same, or very similar, events. We must remember them all, for whether they came back whole, wounded or paid the ultimate price, certainly none remained unmarked. These tales are not recounted in the piecemeal haphazard way in which they were discovered, but more in relation to their own time line simply to make those parts of his story less disjointed and more readable.

The only minor departure from the truth, as I know it, is that the names of all persons still alive at the time of writing have not been given in full in order to respect the wish for privacy expressed by some of their number.

# Chapter 1

## A Sad and Lonely Place

In an unmarked grave in Everton Cemetery there lies buried a long forgotten tale of love and loss, daring and despair, triumph and tragedy. Only now, more than 35 years after he was laid to rest here, can I tell you this man's fascinating story. So whose mortal remains were placed there on the third of January 1985, alone and unremarked with neither friend nor relative to mourn his passing? A war hero, a father, a husband, someone's son. An incredibly lucky and yet a desperately unfortunate soul. A typically unique individual much like any of the rest of us.

How and why did I get to know his story? Well, that is a story in itself, and it began on an ordinary, boring sort of a day.

# Chapter 2

## An Appeal for Help

July 14th 2018        An article on the BBC News website caught my attention. Gregory Delbrouck was asking for help to trace anyone with a connection to an RAF veteran who was shot down over Belgium at the beginning of June 1942, he was the only survivor from the seven man crew of a Lancaster bomber.

Whilst sorting through his late great aunt's effects Gregory had discovered some articles and notes about her work for the Comet Escape Line during the war, a period which Joséphine Van Durme would never discuss.

In particular he had found a set of RAF Air Gunner's wings, and a bloodied scrap of uniform shirt sleeve with the lump of shrapnel that had caused that wound. From Joséphine Van Durme's detailed notes, which she had made at the time and a thank-you letter

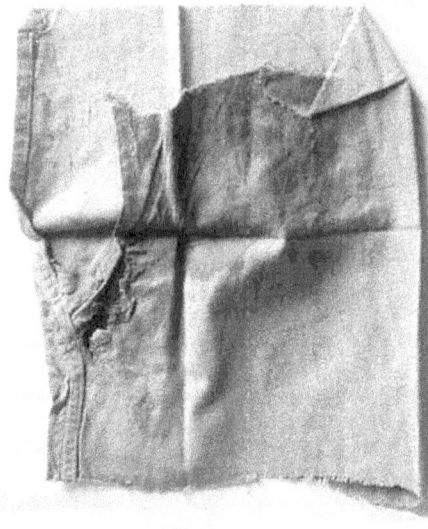

These small clues were found in Josephine Van Durme's effects by Gregory Delbrouck

written in Welsh signed by W R Griffiths. He knew that these belonged to a William Roch Griffiths whom he had discovered had lived at some time in Barmouth North Wales and died in Fazackerly hospital long after the war, but Gregory had been unable to find any living relatives.

Now tracing people from the merest scraps of information is what keeps me doing genealogical research, the satisfaction of uncovering the who, why, when and where that nobody else knows. Besides which no hero should pass in such unremarked circumstances, though sadly far too many do. I was in complete agreement with Gregory; this chap should not be one of those.

With such a distinctive middle name I thought that this would be quite straight forward. (Bad Assumption number 1) A few hours rooting around in some dusty documents, and we would have his family tree all worked out. (Bad Assumption number 2) Then finding some living relatives would follow quite easily. I don't want to labour the point, but this was Bad Assumption number 3, and it would by no means be the last! I sent off an e-mail to the BBC asking them to pass on my contact details to Gregory Delbrouck.

17th July            Feeling very disappointed at having heard nothing after three days, I did an internet search for Gregory, and found a very similar article in the Cambrian Times printed on the 9th July. Being keen to get on with finding William Griffiths' relatives, I e-mailed them too, and had a telephone call from their reporter within the hour. He passed my details on to Gregory who e-mailed me the same evening with a warm welcome and some useful information that he had already uncovered.

Now I had a copy of William's death certificate, and from the

National Archive in Kew, a couple of reports that he had made to MI9 after his return to the UK at the end of July 1942. The first one was a combat report describing the events that occurred during his last fateful mission, and the other recounted his evasion and eventual arrival in Gibraltar. He had also sent an account of his adventures behind enemy lines from the archives of the Comète Line.

This Belgian article was a recent work published on line by researchers of the Réseau Comète (English translation: Comet Network). This was an organised way of transferring allied military personnel back to the UK through occupied territory operated by Belgian civilians opposed to the German occupying forces. William's journey would be through Belgium, France and then over the Pyrenees to 'neutral' Spain, a long and hazardous trip which would take him five weeks.

This would involve many brave escape line members who put their lives at risk in the hope of a better future for their homelands. Many of those would not live to see that happen. They were a vital part of our hero's tale, and his life would have turned out completely differently but for their help. But we are running too far ahead of ourselves. We've got to discover how he came to be there first, before we can find out how the Comet Line had helped to get him back home, and what happened to him after that.

Time for me to get to work.

# Chapter 3

## And So It Begins

The information on his death certificate was exactly what I needed to make a start. As well as the date and cause of his death on the 17th December 1984, it gave his date of birth as the 25th of January 1921, confirmed that he served in the RAF, and the place he was living at the time. And it was sad reading.

William had been living in a hostel for homeless men in Fazackerly. Not really a fit end for a war hero. The informant on the death certificate was a Jill Duffy, and her qualification to report the death was recorded as 'causing the body to be buried'. She was neither a relative nor even a friend but probably an employee of either Fazackerly hospital where he died, or the Field Lane Centre where he had been living, and she was just doing a sad part of her job. Since she did not know much about our man, I would have to remain mindful of the fact that the details given may not have been entirely accurate.

Hoping to discover some more background information about William Roch Griffiths I decided it would be worth spending a little time trying to trace her. A look through the area's records gave me just one possible birth and subsequent marriage for a lady of the right name and age bracket. I found a Facebook page in her married name and so I sent her a message, but I never heard back. Dead end. A pity as she may have had some small scrap of information, maybe even a clue from his effects.

The official records show where he was, when and what

happened to him, but the smallest piece of personal knowledge from someone who was there at the time can lead on to understanding why he was there. With that possible short cut blocked, I was going to have to do it all in the usual way and go to the publically available civil records.

From a quick read through one of the reports he made on his return to England to MI9 I also knew his home address in Barmouth, with that and his date of birth I was able to find him on the 1939 register. This was a real piece of luck; his entry there should have been blacked out.

The 1939 Register was undertaken in September 1939 and the information was then used to give each UK resident Identity and Ration Cards. The register was also later used from 1948 onwards to provide everyone with a National Health Service number and card, and that meant it would have had to have been kept up to date. Deaths and changes of name due to marriage were often noted on the register over the years. When the register was released for public search in 2018 the entries for anyone less than 100 years old were supposed to be redacted and blacked out unless the entry had been altered to signify that the person had already died, then that redaction would not be required.

William's entry should have been hidden but was not, simply because his entry had been corrected from W Richard Griffiths to William Richard Griffiths. The person transcribing the record must have simply assumed that he had died.

Mistakes made by transcribers and indexers are unfortunately not that rare, and can be the absolute bane of any genealogical researcher's life. They can all too frequently prove to be a complete dead end, leaving no way of finding a path back to the original document. Just once in a while though the luck runs the other way. This was both good and bad news for me. I no longer had the unusual middle name to work with, but I now knew where he was and what he did for a living. Also the birth dates on the 1939 Register and on the death certificate were the same.

This is not always the so, even when a close relative is the informant on the death certificate the date can be a year out. Quite common occurrence for elderly people, but when the informant is a stranger, as in William's case, the date can be even more of a guess. Interestingly in the 1939 Register he was listed in the home of an Edward Thomas Humphreys and his wife Mary Ellen; we will be meeting both of them again very shortly.

Now that I had a confirmed birth date, and area, I quickly found a likely birth registration. William R Griffiths registered in the first quarter of 1921 in the Dolgellau registration district with a mother's maiden name of Davies. There was a marriage of a Morris Griffiths to Mary Ellen Davies in 1918, which made them the most likely candidates from the several Griffiths-Davies marriages in the area to be his parents.

This was pretty much confirmed when I found the death of Morris Griffiths recorded in 1926, and the marriage three years later of Mary Ellen Griffiths to Edward Thomas Humphreys, which would explain why William was living with them at the same address in Barmouth on the 1939 register. There was even a very likely looking marriage in 1946 of a William R Griffiths to a Katie Hughes in the area to check out later.

I should explain to any readers unfamiliar with this kind of research that the Civil Registration of vital records started in England and Wales on the third quarter of 1837 (that is 1st July to 30th September) Scotland followed with a slightly different system a little later, and Ireland later still. Birth, Marriage and Death certificates are not available to search; only the indexes to these records. These list the names, dates and places, but not in full detail.

The names are listed as first given name in full, then any other given names as initials only, though this changes from time to time and the second given name is listed in full more often after 1866, second initials again become more common after 1910 until around 1966. Some indexed entries give no clue at all as to a given name.

In the case of a birth registration it was not even compulsory to register the child with a given name, the parents may not have decided at the time and some considered it unlucky to do so until the child had been baptised. There has always been a mechanism to change the given name within a year of registration, though it is very rare to see that has been done.

The dates and places on the indexes are not precise either. The place listed is always the name of the Registration District, which could encompass many towns and villages some with their own Register Offices, sometimes overlapping county boundaries. The dates for marriages are usually accurate to the quarter, since the certificate is made out and a copy handed to the happy couple at the time, but that still spans three months.

Deaths are almost always registered within a few days, because unless the death has been registered no official burial or cremation can take place, but this can still put the event into the quarter after it occurred. An inquest could delay the

14

registration too, as always the date in the index will be shown as the date it was registered, not the date when the event actually took place.

For births the picture is even less certain. The birth should be registered within six weeks. Thus almost half of the births in any quarter could have occurred during the previous one, and for the January to March period that means the previous year. It is sometimes the case that someone making a late registration gave the birth date as just within the six week limit to avoid the small fine that would otherwise have been due. Not helpful for the researcher.

To list all of the problems would take a small book of its own, well perhaps a large book. Since that is not what we are here for, we had better get back to our story.

We already have the bare beginnings of William's family tree and the story of his early years. Just five years old when his father died, so not the best start in life. His Mum manages alone for a few years and then re-marries. There was no way I could have known at the time just how much this simple every day event would complicate the search over the coming months.

While I waited for the birth certificate I've ordered to turn up, I was planning to see if I could find some brothers and sisters, or perhaps some half siblings. Not too bad for a couple of hours work.

# Chapter 4

## Life on Skid Row

18th July                    I e-mailed Gregory with what I've found so far. He is delighted, and impressed that I've done so well so quickly. He has also found the name of the charity that was running the Field Lane Centre where William was living just prior to his admission to Fazackerly hospital, and he too had noticed the possible marriage to Katie Hughes.

20th July                    Still looking for any kind of personal clues, or a short cut, I decided to try to find out more about his time at the Field Lane Centre. It was not as easy as I had hoped. There was a lot of confusion concerning the actual buildings. During the Second World War they had been used as the headquarters and barracks for an RAF Barrage Balloon detachment, and they continued to be used by the RAF for various other purposes until the 1950s. Much of the information available on-line indicated that they had then became a home for ex-RAF personnel.

That may have been true, but by the 1960s the place was being used by the local charity that Gregory had indentified to provide a refuge for homeless men of all sorts. Some were, by coincidence, ex-RAF and other military services but the charity had made no distinction in that respect. Sadly that charity had ceased to operate.

In looking for information that could help me find anything useful I spent a lot of time and effort on false leads. While dead ends, misleading trails and false leads are not that uncommon in this sort of research, I little realised at the time that this was to become such a frequent occurrence.

I eventually found out that the Liverpool Housing Trust had taken on the same role with an entirely new, purpose built centre in the locality. On the telephone the hostel manager told me that they were a completely different entity and had no access to any records from the time I was interested in.

However, one of their volunteers used to work at the Field Lane Centre before it had closed. He would be in to do his shift on the following Monday and I would be able to talk to him directly. I might yet get to learn something useful.

23rd July          I spoke to my new contact from the old Field Lane Centre, and he confirmed that to his certain knowledge, no records still existed. He had not worked there until quite some time after William's death, so could not give me any specific information about him, but almost all of their clients had somewhat chaotic lifestyles.

All of them were unemployed. All were single men, or if they had been married then the marriage had broken down. Many had problems with alcohol and some with petty crime too. If they were violent or too disruptive they would have been encouraged to move on elsewhere. The idea being to give those who were making an effort to get their lives back on track a better chance of success.

William was obviously very down on his luck, but it appears that he was at least making an effort to get his life back into some semblance of normality to have been allowed to stay there. I was not looking forward to finding out what had happened to bring him down so low, but still felt that he should be better remembered for his service to his country, and his story should be told.

# Chapter 5

## Our Man's Beginnings

26th July          The birth certificate arrived, and confirmed that I had the right man and the names of his parents were indeed Morris and Mary Ellen. So I e-mailed Greg. I had found no likely looking half siblings, but then Mary Ellen was 42 when she married for the second time. I did have a list of half a dozen possible brothers and sisters, all showing the mother's maiden name of Davies on the Birth Register Indexes.

They certainly could not all be the right family with some of the dates being far too close together, and there were several Griffiths-Davies couples in the area. Still, I was not expecting more than one or two considering William Richard Griffiths' parents were only married for a little over six years. Even so, I was quietly optimistic. There was also that very likely looking marriage to Katie Hughes at about the time William would have returned home from his war duties. It was all starting to look very promising. Next I needed to eliminate some of these possible siblings from our enquiries and sort out precisely who belonged to our family.

This time I was going to do things slightly differently. I usually order certificates direct from the GRO online, I can do this out of office hours and it's a reliable service, it can take a few days, up to three weeks since I would be asking for a check on the father's name as Morris Griffiths. That is not usually in issue, but I was very keen to get this project off to a good start, I wanted my answers as soon as possible.

If the certificate is from a Register Office close to my home I will often travel there and hope that they will provide a 'while you wait' service, and if they are not too busy with a block of weddings and a queue of folk needing to register events then they usually do. The office I needed was too far away for that, but they had published their e-mail address and telephone number.

I sent an e-mail with the outline of the whole story of William Richard Griffiths' adventures and details of my six prime candidates asking for any help that they could give, and I immediately received a reply. An automated reply. The staff member who dealt with historical records was on holiday until the weekend, she would get back to me on the following Monday on her return.

It looked like I had made a bad call. Still I did not really want to do too much more work until I've definitely got the right parents for William, and I already had a busy weekend planned, so I ordered the marriage certificates for William R Griffiths to Katie Hughes in 1946 specifying Morris Griffiths as father of the groom, and Morris Griffiths to Mary Ellen Davies in 1918 from the GRO on-line after all.

30th July                  Early on the next Monday morning I received an e-mail from the Register Office, my contact there was back at work, and would I ring her? On the telephone I explained that I was looking for living relatives of William Richard Griffiths, and told her the outlines of his story as I knew it. She was immediately intrigued, she had an interest in family history and was actively building her own family tree. Now to be asked to help find out about a local lad who had some amazing adventures during his RAF career was like a flame to a moth, she was as hooked as I was.

Firstly she confirmed that that the marriage certificate for his parents that I have already ordered, but would not arrive for about another 10 days or so, was the right one. Strictly speaking she did not actually confirm that, for to do so would have been against the disclosure rules. But she told me I would not have to continue looking for a different marriage! I like subtle.

I then gave her my list of six possible other children that could have belonged to this couple. If indeed any were the children of Morris and Mary Ellen I would buy copies of those certificates on the spot. She then went delving into the records to check them all out. A couple of hours later I got a call back from her.

Not a single one of the possible children on my list were part of Morris Griffiths and Mary Ellen Davies' family, nor was she able to find any others that were not included on my list. Furthermore she told me that Morris Griffiths is not recorded as the father of the William R Griffiths that married Katie Hughes in 1946, and that chap's name was not William Richard Griffiths. Nor could she find a William Richard whose father's name was Morris marrying in her registration district between 1937 and 1965. It was beginning to look like William may have been an only child who died without marrying and leaving children of his own.

Not a wasted call though, I had at least made a very useful contact that I would need again before this search was over, and I now knew that if I was going to find a marriage I would have to look further afield.

4th August          The picture was looking considerably less promising than it had done just a week or so earlier. With no probable children or siblings for William Richard Griffiths discovered so far, I was left with trying to trace Morris and

Mary Ellen's siblings. His uncles, aunts and his cousins would know less about him, but I might still be able to pick up some clues as to whom he may have married, when and where. I would have to go back a generation to find them.

I found Morris without too much trouble on the 1901 census. His birth date of around 1894 and his father's name of John Griffiths would be confirmed by his marriage certificate which should arrive in a few days. He was living with parents John and Anne and five brothers in a small village just a few miles north of Barmouth. His father John was a joiner. Both John and Anne had been born around 1852.

I also managed to find John and Anne with their four eldest children on the 1891 census. They were still living in Llanenddwyn. With them was a William Jones listed as Anne's uncle. John and Anne's eldest child, Griffith Jones Griffiths had been born around 1881. On the 1901 census he was a farmer. His middle name practically confirmed his mother's family name.

I soon found John Griffiths marrying an Anne Jones early in 1880 with Griffith Jones Griffiths born to the couple just over a year later. I was really hoping by this stage not to have to go any deeper in to their past family history. Sorting out exactly which John Griffiths and which Anne Jones they were from the many possible candidates in that area would have taken a lot of time and effort.

Their second son, a blacksmith in 1901, was John Griffiths born in late 1882. Robert Griffiths was born in 1884 and was a Railway Station Clerk in 1901. Brother Richard, born in early 1886 was a shoe maker according to the 1901 census. He had died in 1909, and I could find no marriage record for him. Then there were the last two children, William, who was born in mid 1889, was still at school with Morris on the 1901 census.

With Robert being the least common name among the local Griffiths families, and also because he had administered his father's estate in 1933, I researched him first. He had married an Elizabeth Griffith in 1918. The pair was on the 1939 Register living in Dolgellau where Robert was the Station Master. There were no named children living with them, and no redacted lines for the household which could have been children born after 1918, nor could I find likely looking candidates on the Birth Register Indexes. I was confident that they had had no children.

5th August                    Researching Griffith Jones Griffiths turned into a long hard slog, and for precisely no reward. I found him easily enough on the 1911 census living in the Toxteth area of Liverpool and working as a Joiner, although there were other Griffith Griffiths' on the 1911 census he was the only one from Llanenddwyn. He recorded himself as married, but was living alone. On the 1911 census married women were instructed to note the length of the marriage, the number of children from that marriage born alive and the number of children still living. Griffith filled this part in, though he was not supposed to; this was not an uncommon occurrence on the 1911 census.

He had declared the marriage to have taken place five years previously, there had been only one child and he or she was still alive at the time of the census. That had, of course, been crossed out as he was not a married woman. But I could still read it plainly enough and I therefore knew that there was a child to be found who would have been a cousin to William, I would just have to track this family down.

I could find only one possible marriage, to an Elizabeth Jones in Toxteth in mid 1905, followed very shortly after by a birth of Henry Ifor Griffiths on the 8th August. Since I had already seen Henry Ifor Griffiths of the same age living with his grandparents John and Anne back home in Llanenddwyn on the 1911 census, that all tied up very neatly. Next I had to find out if Henry Ifor had married and had any surviving offspring. It took quite a while to find any more information at all. I had hoped that would have been easier, it was a reasonably unusual middle name, which usually means a lot less cross checking and fewer false leads to rule out.

Eventually I turned up some clues that he might have gone to America. After some searching there I unearthed his application for US citizenship in 1927, and I also found that his parents were both living with him there on the 1925 US census. I could find no other children for them. Henry Ifor died in 1976 and I could find no evidence that he ever married, and since any of his offspring would have been second cousins to William, and lived an ocean apart, I could not see that they would be likely to know much about his life. Two down with no possibility of surviving family to contact.

That left me with two more uncles on his father's side of the family to track down, John and William. With a common family name of Griffiths, and common given names, I knew that this could well turn out to be very hard work. I would need to be able to know for certain that I was following the right man. This would entail tying together several pieces of evidence. All I had so far was a birth date and place. The obvious first place to look was the 1939 Register, which does have full birth dates that would provide confirmation that I had the right chaps if I also bought the birth certificates. By 1939 they may well have married with children of their own, giving a path to possible living relatives. I could find neither of the brothers there.

I also checked on the available military records as both were in the right age group to have served in World War 1. There were several possible deaths for either man, but none of these records had any details of their next of kin or home address.

After several days of checking and cross checking records for all of the possible John and William Griffiths in the area I was absolutely no further forward, I knew that I would have to buy a fair few marriage and death certificates to make any progress with these two. I spent some time making detailed notes, just in case I had to pick up these threads again later. For now, I would have to shift my attention to Mary Ellen Davies' family and hope for better luck there. With even more Davies families in the area I knew that this could turn out to be even more complicated.

# Chapter 6

## Making a Start on His Family Tree

8th August          From the Birth Register Indexes and Census records from 1891, 1901 and 1911 there were only two women called Mary Ellen Davies of the right age living in the area, one living in Penrhyndeudraeth and another living in Corwen with her parents William Robert and Catherine Elizabeth, both places were in the Ffestiniog registration district.

Since the Penrhyndeudraeth one looked the more likely of the two I decided to try and rule the other out as being a part of our family first. That was fairly easily done, I found a marriage record for her to a William M John in Corwen in 1920, and then found them as a couple on the 1939 Register living in Cardiff, which confirmed her birth date as 1887. Since our Mary Ellen was born in 1886, and was already married to Morris Griffiths by 1920, I was sure that she was the Mary Ellen still living in Penrhyndeudraeth and I would be following the right family.

The General Register Office birth indexes had shown that Mary Ellen's mother's maiden name was Williams, and from the 1891 census her parents were listed as William and Mary Ann. I found records for William Davies and Mary Ann Williams marrying in early 1886, with Mary Ellen being born on the 11th of November that same year. By the time of the 1911 census Mary Ellen was the eldest of eight children.

The next one of her siblings was Catherine Davies, also known as Kate, born in mid 1888. Then along came brothers James in 1890, William in 1895 and Robert born in 1897.

25

The next was her sister Gwen born in 1899, then brothers Ellis Parry in 1902 and finally Emrys in 1905.

Since James, Ellis Parry and Emrys were all on the 1939 Register as single and still living with their mother Mary Ann I did not hold out much hope of finding any descendants from them. So Gwen would be next to research, and at the time I did not appreciate that this was to be such a frustrating tale full of twists and turns that would take many months to resolve.

I searched for Gwen Davies born around 1899 and found only two in the right area; the other being born in 1897 and she appeared on the later censuses in Trawsfynydd. There were three possible marriages, in 1921, 1925 and 1934. By checking the birth dates of these three women in the 1939 register under their married names, it was evident that our Gwen Davies married Aneurin Ioan Harries in 1934 and was still living in Penrhyndeudraeth in 1939. There was a redacted person living in the same household, which would usually indicate someone born between 1918 and the end of September 1939. At last. A possible link to the present day.

Fairly straightforward so far, now I thought, if I could just find out who Aneurin and Gwen's children were and what became of them it could unlock the whole story. And in a way I was right, but certainly not in a way that I had expected. This mystery would get much deeper before it was to be resolved.

9th August              A long and very frustrating search failed to turn up even the slightest hint of any children for Gwen and Aneurin. Nothing in the Birth Register Indexes. Nothing in the Church and Parish registers. No mentions in the school admission rolls. And I was checking for all sorts of variations in names to find any misspellings or transcription errors. Nothing. Yet I was sure there should be at least one child, which would fit in with the redacted line on the 1939 census.

Could he or she be one of the very few whose birth was never registered? I doubted that very much. Aneurin was a School Teacher in 1939, surely not the sort of chap to forget, or choose to ignore the requirement to register a birth. The entry could perhaps be for a 'live in' servant; if he, or more likely she, was under 20 years old the entry would have been blacked out. This was a possibility, since Aneurin was 34 at the time and as school teacher, he may have been able to afford a servant. But they were going out of fashion by the time of the 1939 Register. I remained certain that there was a child living with the Harries family, but I had no idea who that child could be.

12th August               Although I remained convinced that Gwen and Aneurin held the key to finding a cousin for William, I was obviously getting nowhere. Time, I felt, that I had to move on to Gwen's siblings. I filled in some more details of their part of the family tree, some addresses and the dates of their deaths, and made notes of the things I had uncovered so far. I was especially careful to note what I had ruled out, to save covering the same ground later. I then made a start on Gwen's younger sister Kate. Inconveniently she had been registered as Catherine, but appeared in all the relevant censuses as Kate. I needed therefore to check both names for everything.

I did come across a likely marriage for her, and found both her and her husband on the 1939 Register. But it was a late marriage made in 1926 when Kate was 38. Any children born to the couple would have been under 13 at the time of the 1939 Register, and I would have expected them to be young enough to be still living with their parents. But there were no children at their address, nor any redacted lines that could have been children. I found no likely possibilities on the Birth Indexes either. Another dead end. That left me with the two remaining brothers, William and Robert.

I expected these two to be no easier to research than the Griffiths brothers I had had to give up on at the beginning of the month. I was right. There were several possible marriages, and deaths for each man, and after a day of intense cross checking, I was unable to show which I should be following. Three days and not a single step closer to a living relative. Time once again to make my notes and seek an entirely new approach.

# Chapter 7

## Down the Garden Path

17th August          I was still waiting to hear from the GRO about William Richard Griffiths' 'wrong' marriage certificate to Katie Hughes. So I decided to check on the progress of my order. It was marked as being posted that very morning, which I knew from past experience, actually meant passed on to the despatch area for posting, so may still take a day or two to arrive. Now I really was confused. Either the GRO were sending me a certificate they knew I did not want, or they had found the right one in an area I did not ask them to look, perhaps my friendly Registrar had made a mistake and it was the right one after all.

As I had already found two possible daughters for the marriage, and with no other promising looking leads to follow, I picked up those threads to find out what happened to them. Since both had fairly unusual names the research was easy. The eldest had lived in the area until 2010 without marrying and then disappeared from the available records, except for a probate record dated 2013 in her maiden name. I could expect to find no surviving offspring for her.

The younger daughter had married, and her married name was a nice easy one to work with. I found her and her husband Graham on the electoral rolls in North Wales, and their telephone number. Half an hour later I had her story. She confirmed that her sister had never married and died in 2013, they were indeed the daughters of the Katie Hughes who had married in 1946, but to a William Robert Griffiths. Not my man, and a whole day wasted. The Registrar had been correct; I would not be needing that marriage certificate.

I still had no real clue whether that was the certificate already in the post to me, or if I was in for a surprise.

18th August             The expected marriage certificate arrived. As I had by then suspected, it was for William Robert Griffiths, whose father was not Morris Griffiths. The bride was indeed Katie Hughes. I had to start the long and tedious process of persuading the GRO to refund what I had paid as this was not the certificate I had ordered. Time to send an update e-mail to Gregory.

At this stage I had the feeling that I was not able to see the wood for the trees. Although I had a fair amount of information to work with, I had stopped making any progress. Since I had found in the past that taking a break from difficult research that never seemed to lead anywhere, concentrating or something else often produced results. It seems that sometimes the mind needs to take a step away from a difficult problem to come up with a new solution. I decided to take a few days off, and follow up on some previously discovered leads for my own family tree. A few easy successes can frequently give a boost to getting more difficult problems sorted out.

In the mean time I had managed to find a website hosting a forum dedicated to 50 and 61 Squadrons of the RAF. I joined, and posted a request for any information available for William Richard Griffiths' time there, and the circumstances surrounding the loss of the aircraft that he was in on the night of June 2/3rd 1942.

# Chapter 8

## The Mystery Photograph

19th August        Greg e-mailed a reply to tell me that he had a visit from the Comtesse Madame d'Oultremont who had heard the story of his search for W R Griffiths. She was president of the official "Comète Line Remembrance" organisation and knew that Gregory's great aunt served the Comet Line during WW2 alongside her own father and uncle. She had asked him to pass on a message of thanks and encouragement to me. That was a pleasant and unexpected surprise; it's not every day that you get thanks from a countess.

He also mentioned a photograph that he had recently found in his aunt's possessions. Uniquely this one was not attached to any notes and had no name on it, Joséphine Van Durme was usually far better organised than that. After asking around he had found the daughter of one of Joséphine's Comet Line colleagues. She was a young teenager at the time and she remembered William

The photo of William 'Roch' Griffiths found in Joséphine Van Durme's effects.
Courtesy of Gregory Delbrouck

31

as tall and slim with brown hair and 'not bad looking' briefly passing through their home.

She felt that the picture could well be him. Gregory thought that the photograph must have been taken in Belgium in order to produce the necessary fake ID papers that were so vital to a successful escape. He was not entirely correct, though that was often done. The mystery of this mystery photograph would not be fully solved for a further 10 months! And there would be other mystery photographs to puzzle over as the search progressed.

27th August                    I decided that I could no longer put off the search for all marriages for a William R Griffiths between 1939 and 1970 anywhere in England or Wales. I chose the start date because I knew that he was still single and living with his mother and stepfather on the 1939 Register, and if he married after 1970 he was unlikely to have had any children. I found 83. Far too many to start the process of applying for the marriage certificates a few at a time specifying that the Groom's father's given name must be Morris.

In an effort to reduce that number I then looked to see if I could find a William R Griffiths who had been born between 18 and 30 years before each of the marriages in the same locality, and would therefore be a much more likely candidate than our William R Griffiths. This was a long, boring and laborious process that eventually reduced my list to around 30. I felt that I would need to reduce these possibilities still further before applying for any marriage certificates.

Since it was still common for children to be named after their relatives at that time, and I had a fairly good grasp on

William's immediate family member's names, I considered that it was worth checking the forenames of the children that would have been associated to some of these marriages. I would have been particularly interested to find a Morris or an Ifor, but found neither. I realised that what I needed was a firmer idea of both when and where to look for a marriage for William Richard Griffiths.

# Chapter 9

## Off to Join the Forces

2nd September        Over the weekend I received an e-mail from Greg. He had obtained a copy of William's RAF service record. All the information that could be described as personal had been blanked out because Gregory was not a close relative, and of course that covered everything we were most interested in finding out. But there was a lot of information on where he was, when, and what he was tasked with; we would just have to work with what we had got.

I had a quick look at his war time career and found that his initial training was carried out at RAF Cardington from 16th December 1940. I had lived within walking distance of the RAF station there for ten years; he may well have had a pint or two in the Turnpike, which had been my local pub! His first assignment was to Number 5 Mechanical Transport Company on 17th June 1941.

That unit's role was to transport crated aircraft to Liverpool docks for their sea voyage out to the various overseas squadrons. His duties were not detailed; he could have been a lorry driver, or driver's mate, a motor mechanic or just a general dogsbody. But he had fallen on his feet; it was an 'easy number', a safe and honourable way to 'do your bit'.

This does not appear to have been enough for our hero, because by the 9th of August the same year he was at Number 9 Air Gunnery School. He had volunteered for Bomber Command and was really going to get into the fight for his country. On 7th of October he moved on to 25 Operational Training Unit at Finningley to further hone his new skills and get to grips with flying and fighting at night.

He would quickly have realized his 'easy ticket' was now well and truly cancelled when he was introduced to the much disliked Hampden and the ill-fated Manchester bombers used at 25 OTU during his time there. He was then posted to 61 Squadron based at North Luffenham on 8th February 1942. He had been in the RAF for 14 months and was about to get seriously involved in the war!

When William joined 61 Squadron it was equipped with the Avro Manchester two engine bomber, which was the forerunner of the famous Lancaster four engine aircraft, which came to be rightly regarded as the backbone of the Bomber Command fleet.

AUSTRALIAN WAR MEMORIAL                     UK121219

**William's new office. The rear turret of an Avro Manchester, the turret of the Lancaster was practically identical.**

The Manchester was not so good, just the opposite in fact. The Rolls Royce Vulture engines should have been both powerful and efficient, but they were neither. Worse still were they were very unreliable. Problems with the liquid cooling systems meant that they were prone to overheat and loose power, or even seize up and self destruct. Bearing failures and engine fires were also common occurrences.

Bombing tactics at the time brought up yet another problem

35

with these engines. Many pilots thought that to close the engines down, feather the propellers and make a gliding approach onto the target gave the bomber some small advantage. The noise could not be tracked from the ground, so there would be a chance that the anti-aircraft gunners may not open fire. In fact it made no difference at all.

The German defenders did have acoustic detectors which they had used very early in the war, but they had not proved to be effective and by this stage had been replaced by more modern RADAR. But it did mean that the pilot would have to reset the propellers and restart the engines to fly away from the target area. The Vulture engines had a nasty tendency for the feathering gear to stick while the engine was shut down in flight, so the engine would not then provide any forward thrust when restarted. In most cases the Manchester had great difficulty sustaining level flight on just one engine, although it was designed to do so.

With an engine out of action it was just a big, heavy glider looking desperately for somewhere to land.

Somewhere in enemy territory.

In the dark.

While being shot at.

Morale amongst Manchester crews was never high.

# Chapter 10

## We Find His Sister

3rd September        I revisited my attempts to find a possible marriage for William Richard Griffiths, referring to my previous nationwide list. This time I was going to remove any of those marriages that I felt had occurred too far away from any of the places that he was listed as being stationed at in his RAF service records. I hoped that may leave me with less than a handful of possible marriages to check out, but instead I ended up with precisely none. Another half a day's work and still no further forward. I really did need a fresh approach. If he did get married, I had either missed it, or mistakenly ruled it out, or he got married abroad during one of his foreign postings.

This was now really starting to get frustrating. I was left with no leads, nor any clues as to where to go next. But I felt that I had made a promise to Gregory, and also silently to William. Besides which, I could not possibly disappoint a countess and daughter of a hero of the Comet Escape Line. No, I would not be giving up just yet.

I had found before that in complex cases much of what is discovered simply makes things appear more complicated and confusing. Then some insignificant scrap of information suddenly transforms everything, and the answer is obvious. This key to the whole search need not necessarily be new information. It's often something that was discovered quite early on in the process, but had been dismissed as irrelevant, or misinterpreted, or maybe not even noticed because so little of the overall picture had been known at the time.

This was definitely a good time for a recap. I would take the chance to go back and review the steps I had made along the way, and what progress I had managed to make. I needed to spot something I had overlooked or where I might have made a mistake.

4th September          Returning  to  the  searches  of William's aunts and uncles kept leading me back to Gwen Davies. I decided that I really did need to know who was living with her and Aneurin on the 1939 Register. I planned to talk to my friendly registrar the next day; I hoped that perhaps she would be able to find something that I had missed.

5th September          I  had  another  long  phone conversation with my Registrar friend early that afternoon and asked her to confirm that I had not missed any children for Aneurin and Gwen Harries. I also asked her to check, as I had done, for combinations of Harries or Harris with Davies or Davis. Davies and Harries tend to be used in Wales (especially in Welsh speaking areas like Merionethshire) and Davis and Harris in the rest of the UK, though that's not hard and fast rule, and an easy slip of the pen for a registrar to make.

While she was looking through her records, I was also checking things on the web, and it occurred to me that when I had drawn up my list of possible siblings for William R Griffiths I had not checked for any births with a mother's maiden name of DAVIS, only DAVIES. I soon found an Ann Griffiths; born early 1920.

When the registrar returned with the news that she could find no children for Gwen and Aneurin, I mentioned my newly discovered Ann. She quickly checked her records but could find no trace of her birth registration.

A short time later she rang back. She had found Ann. She had been born on the 11th December 1919 but registered in January 1920, with the same father (Morris) and same mother (Mary Ellen), but at the time they were living a few miles from where William had been born.

Now we were starting to get somewhere. All I had to do is find out what happened to William's sister Ann. I did not, at that time, realise exactly how close I had come to the answer to that particular question. It was right under my nose.

When I e-mailed Gregory with the news that I had found William's sister, and the events of his early RAF history he replied that he was very excited. We are on the verge of completing the search. We will have living relatives to contact soon. They would surely know If William did get married and have children; they would soon tell us everything. Remind me dear reader, what Bad Assumption number we are up to now, because I think this makes it at least 4.

I really hoped that he was right, but I was worried that there would be more than enough Ann Griffiths in the area to make this a long search. We had though, at last, made a good move in the right direction.

# Chapter 11

## Unravelling Ann's Life Story

6th September          The very first thing that I found when searching for more records concerning Ann Griffiths was her death in 1987 aged 67. With an exact birth date given on the death indexes at this period which matched precisely, I was worried that she may not have married. But there were still possibilities. This may have been and Ann of unknown maiden name who married a Mr Griffiths and the birth date was entirely co-incidental.

Our Ann also may have married a Mr Griffiths and so not changed her name. And lastly, even if she did not marry, she may still have had some children, but if that was so, they may prove to be very difficult to find. I still had a trail to chase; I just could not shake the feeling that it was not going to be straightforward.

A search for marriages in Merionethshire brought up six possibilities, of which three were in the south of the county. I would check the northern ones first. I ruled out The Annie M record and was similarly not convinced that the next one for an Anne was correct. The third index entry for Ann Griffiths marrying Elwyn T Griffiths in the second quarter of 1947 seemed to me to fit the bill exactly. I ordered this certificate on-line from the GRO, specifying that the bride's father's name must be Morris.

Now I needed to find out a bit more about Elwyn, and try to find some children. But that would have to wait. I was going to be on family duties until the weekend. Typical, just when I have a hot lead which I am desperate to follow, I have some longstanding personal commitments to attend to and have to take a few days off!

10th September    I managed to find just two Elwyn Griffiths' in the area at the time of the 1939 Register, and only one of those was Elwyn Thomas Griffiths. The other one had been born in the south of the county in 1917 and had married an Elizabeth Hughes there in 1942; I felt that I could safely rule him out. Our Elwyn Thomas Griffiths was listed on the register with a birth date of 13th October 1916 living in Penrhyndeudraeth with his sister Iris Jane and their parents, William Morris and Elizabeth. They were on the same page of the register just a few houses away from Gwen and Aneurin Harries and of course the mysterious redacted person.

Extract from the 1939 Register.                    Crown Copyright

I soon found Elwyn's entry on the deaths index for the second quarter of 1985, and I could be reasonably sure it was him

41

because the index entries for that period include the full birth date; and that date matched the one on the 1939 Register. I could not, however, find a birth record in Merionethshire for Elwyn Thomas, nor Iris Jane, or any likely marriage record for their parents.

After some deeper digging around I did turn up a set of records that brought some light onto his father. There was a Birth Index entry in the Penrhyndeudraeth area for William M Griffiths in the second quarter of 1887, which tied in neatly with his known birth date from the 1939 Register of 8th April 1887. I also discovered a corresponding entry on the 1901 census showing him living in Penrhyndeudraeth with his parents William and Jane. But then nothing further in the area until 1939.

Eventually I found William on the 1911 census living as a boarder at 47 Francis Street, Abertridwr in the Pontypridd registration district, nearly 100 miles away in South Wales. His birth place had been transcribed as Penshyndendonett Marssonetshire, but on inspection of the actual image showed it was indeed Penrhyndeudraeth Merionethshire. Yet again a transcriber had done their very best to make sure no one ever found this record, but he would just have to try a bit harder next time. At the same address was a Lizzie Hughes (mistranscribed as Slughes), sister in law to the householder, who had been born in Llanberis in 1882. Llanberis is just a few miles from Penrhyndeudraeth.

I soon turned up an entry in the indexes to the marriage registers for William M Griffiths to Lizzie Hughes in early 1911 in the Pontypridd district which included the village of Abertridwr. I then found the Birth Register Index entries for Iris Jane and Elwyn T in 1911 and 1916, also in the

Pontypridd district, both with the mother's maiden name of Hughes. I ordered PDF copies of these two birth certificates direct from the GRO.

It was, at last, starting to make sense. William Morris Griffiths moved to Abertridwr to try to make his living as a coal miner there, he boarded with a family with origins also in Penrhyndeudraeth, indeed they may well have all gone south together. While there he married a girl from near his home town, and eventually moved back with his wife and children.

With the unusual names of Elwyn Thomas and Iris Jane, I was sure I had the family all worked out correctly. In order to be absolutely certain, I would need to see their birth certificates. It had taken two days of intense searching, and I had had to go back a further generation to Elwyn Thomas Griffiths' grandfather, but I felt satisfied that I was beginning to make proper progress.

Now I had to try and track down any children that Elwyn Thomas and Ann Griffiths had, these would be nephews and nieces to our William Richard Griffiths.

12th September       I then found that there had been over sixty children born in the area to a Griffiths-Griffiths couple. From that long list, three names caught my attention straight away; Ann, Elwyn and William R. All three were born between 1948 and 1955, with birthdates neatly spaced out far enough apart to have been siblings. That just had to be them! Well, actually no, it was not, but I would not discover that for some time yet.

I knew I really ought to have waited for confirmation that these were indeed the children of our Mr and Mrs Griffiths.

But I was hot on the trail, and at the time very busy during the day with family duties, so I would have to wait to get any proof. I decided to continue following these three children. It seemed like a good decision, because I quickly found some good leads for both Elwyn and William R.

Both Elwyn and William had married women with fairly unusual surnames, so I would not have too much difficulty finding their children. In William's case I soon found three children, his eldest son's forename was not sufficiently unusual for me to consider spending too much time following him. The other two children looked to be far more promising.

They also turned out to be very elusive! Even with William's spouse's uncommon forenames, I kept running into records from distant parts of the country which could not possibly be them, unless they managed to get married and onto the electoral rolls while still in their early teens! No progress there then.

Elwyn junior's children however proved to be more straightforward. He had two daughters, the youngest had a set of forenames that made her very easy to trace. Within a couple of evenings I had a marriage for her and an address in Porthmadog. I decided that I needed some confirmation before I attempted to contact her.

17th September        I finally managed to make some free time in office hours and spent some time talking with my friendly Registrar in North Wales. Bad news, all three of my hot leads had been born to different unmarried women named Griffiths. The Index had been wrongly transcribed in every case. They should have appeared as Griffiths-BLANK not Griffiths-Griffiths!

Yet another blind alley. And another chunk of wasted time. I was on the right track with the marriage of Ann to Elwyn Thomas, but there were no likely children on the birth indexes in her area. Once more I was going to have to retrace my steps looking for anything I had previously missed, or take a new approach.

I finally found an Elwyn Thomas Griffiths on someone's tree on Ancestry. I was, and still am, always very wary of the family trees there, I have seen so many that could not possibly be true, and often in ways that defy belief. This one was a private tree, so it told me a person matching the details I have searched for is there, but nothing else. This meant that I could not check for any obvious errors, or try to follow the route that they had used to uncover his history. With few other options I sent the owner of the tree a message. I told her that I wanted to trace Elwyn Thomas Griffith's descendants. I received a reply very promptly.

Elwyn, she said, was a distant relative; she had met him in the past, and would make enquiries of his son when he returned from his holiday the following week. This man would be William Richard Griffith's nephew.

I replied to her and told her the bare outlines of William's RAF adventures, why we were keen to contact living relatives and left my phone number. I could not quite believe this was not yet another false lead, but typically for this whole exercise we then had to sit on our hands and wait. Even more typically this lead was to prove to have a very potent sting in the tail.

# Chapter 12

## A Door Slams Shut

20th September        I spent some time filling in some more details of Ann and Elwyn Thomas' life story. Elwyn had worked as a clerk at the explosives manufacturing site just outside Penrhyndeudraeth and had died in 1985, Ann died just two years later. I e-mailed Gregory with a full update.

25th September        I picked up an e-mail from Greg in the evening. It included a copy of Mary Ellen Davies' death certificate that had been sent to him by another researcher, Di. I had no idea until then that anyone else was attempting to assist Gregory in our epic quest. I had previously been very impressed with everything that he had uncovered, I was sure I could not have produced the records that he had found in a foreign country. Now though, his secret was out!

The address on the death certificate was in Penrhyndeudraeth, but gave Mary Ellen's usual home address as 1 Mount Pleasant in Barmouth, which was where she was living with her second husband and son William in 1939. The informant was A I Harries of School House Penrhyndeudraeth and he gave his relationship as 'Brother in Law'. He was, of course her sister Gwen's husband Anuerin Ioan Harries.

This all reminded me yet again that I had been unable to find Ann Griffiths in the 1939 Register records. She was not living with her mother and stepfather in Barmouth, and I had found her nowhere else. Since I now knew that she married in 1947 she would have been listed under her birth name, and there was a chance that her entry may have been amended with her married name and not redacted. Looking back, I can see that I had more than enough clues to be able to work out where she was, but I just could not figure it out at the time. I would get another huge clue the next day. But even then, I still did not see it.

26th September          The marriage certificate for Ann and Elwyn Thomas Griffiths arrived in the post late in the morning, and I had an e-mail from the GRO that I had some certificates ready to download from there too. They were Elwyn Thomas and Iris Jane's birth certificates that I had been waiting for since the 17th of the month. They were all as I had been expecting. I did notice that Ann's address was given as Bryniau Hendre, Penrhyndeudaeth on the marriage certificate, which I thought that I had seen somewhere before, but could not place. I had a brief look through my notes on Ann's family, but I could not immediately find it. I should have looked a lot harder.

I then checked on the ancestry trees for Iris Jane Griffiths, born 1911 in Pontypridd and later living in Penrhyndeudraeth. It turned up a match in the same private family tree where I had found Elwyn Thomas. So I now knew that we were certainly both researching the same family. Naturally I sent her a follow up message detailing everything I had just proved that morning and asked if she had managed to contact Elwyn's son. A man she actually knew. The very same chap that we were trying so hard to find.

I also asked her to pass on my address, e-mail address and telephone number to this mystery chap. Again I would have to wait for her reply. When it finally came, it was certainly not what I had been hoping for.

6th October          I finally received a reply from

Elwyn's relative. She had not contacted his son, and gave no reasons for that. She had instead talked the whole thing over with some of her cousins. Between them they had concluded that I was looking at the wrong family. Their Elwyn Thomas Griffiths had married a woman called Nanw, who was from the Harris family, and could not possibly be the same person as William R Griffiths' sister Ann. The fact that I had the marriage certificate to hand, Elwyn and his sister Iris' birth certificates and his parent's marriage details all made no difference. I must be wrong. I was not, as events would later prove, but that would make no difference, she would not be persuaded.

I have used other people's trees on Ancestry in my research in the past. As I have previously said, I knew that many, if not most, were more works of fiction than fact; often containing really impossible scenarios. I had seen women listed as having given birth to three children on different dates and places many miles apart all in the same year, a mother aged just six when her first child was born and over sixty when the last one came along, children born several years after their mother had died: I could go on for pages. But this was a completely new slant on the problem. We were researching the same family, but even when presented with documentary proof, she simply would not believe it. I would get no further correspondence from her. That would extend the search by a good two months!

She had however confirmed that, at least according to her possibly unreliable tree, there was someone to find, and given me another massive clue, but that was just a little too well hidden for me to spot at the time.

I knew that I had to reduce the list of Griffiths - Griffiths children in the area to a more manageable number, for now I could at least concentrate only on the males, but that still left 40 names to sort through. Once I had reduced this list of possibilities a lot more then I would be able to enlist the help of my favourite registrar to find him. It was not going to be an easy job.

# Chapter 13

## William Goes to War

8th October          I had received some replies to my questions on the 61 Squadron forum. These did not bring any personal information to light as I had hoped, but I now had some small insight into his time there. Someone kindly posted the Operational Record Book entry of his final flight on the 2nd June 1942. It was the usual very stark 'The crew took off and nothing further was heard.'

I wanted to know a lot more than that!

10th October          Having seen copy of the entry from the Operations Record Book for Sergeant Griffiths' last flight in Lancaster R5613 on the Squadron 61 forum, I obtained copies of the Operations Record Books from the National Archive for all of the time that William was there to help me to understand his operational career in more detail. They made a fascinating read.

His first operation on the 24th February 1942 was a trip to Paris to drop leaflets. This was typical; a new crew's first operation would usually be a 'milk run', a target with light defences and little strategic importance. This trip was a five hour flight in Manchester L7497, mostly above the cloud cover and no opposition was encountered.

The crew consisted of the Pilot Ralph Edward Clark, 2nd Pilot Stanley Holmes Lincoln who was a New Zealander, Navigator Edward Ernest Patchett, Wireless Operator Alastair Macnab McKelvie, 2nd Wireless Operator/Front Gunner D C Davies, 1st Air Gunner D T King, and William as the rear gunner. They had all been posted together on the 8th February from 25 Operational Conversion Unit where they had trained together as a crew. There is more information about these brave lads in Appendix I.

Both Clark and McKelvie were very experienced, having flown in the smaller Hampdens with 144 Squadron for some time and both had earned a Distinguished Flying Medal. Lincoln had flown as second pilot to the squadron leader just once a few days previously, a trip normally undertaken by the new pilot to familiarise him to combat conditions. This was their first operational flight together.

Avro Manchester in flight.          Model and photo courtesy of Hal MacDonald.

Although the entry in the 61 Squadron Operations Record Book gives the take off as being from North Luffenham, the squadron operated the Manchester aircraft from their satellite airfield at Woolfox Lodge about five miles away until they later moved to Syerston. William's next sortie was on March 10th from Woolfox to Essen to bomb the Krupps works in Manchester L7516 and was with the same crew. This was the

51

reserve aircraft, the one allocated for the trip being unserviceable, an all too common occurrence with the Manchester. The trip of over five hours was unremarkable and they landed at Waddington due to poor visibility at their home station.

Trip number three was not so uneventful and underlined why the Manchester was not well regarded. The same crew took off from Woolfox at 21:40 on the 28th of March in Manchester R5786 to go to Lubeck. The official language of the report made on their return does not adequately convey the drama that unfolded that night.

'Had difficulty maintaining height until 2 bombs jettisoned off the English coast' roughly translates as: The aircraft struggled to get airborne due to one, or possibly both, Vulture engines being unable to produce full power. Attempts to climb to a safe height to clear obstacles in the flight path risked losing too much airspeed and stalling.

Crashing even from a low height with a full fuel and bomb load would not have had a good outcome. With little height, and not much airspeed, manoeuvring would have been a very delicate and dangerous undertaking, the slower the aircraft flies and the tighter it turns the more height it will inevitably lose. Returning to base and attempting a landing would also have been seen as too dangerous for the same reasons. A direct heading for the nearest part of the coast avoiding any high ground while making as few extremely gentle, shallow turns as possible would have been their only reasonable option.

Once safely out to sea they had some choices, jettison all of the bombs and come home, drop some of the bombs and see if the lightened aircraft was then flyable and either come home and attempt a risky landing with a part bomb load or continue the mission. They chose the latter, dropped half of the bombs in one of the designated jettison areas of the North Sea and went off to war in an already wounded aeroplane.

'Bombs dropped from 5,600 feet in a shallow dive' five and a half thousand feet is a very uncomfortable place to be over a target. A low flying aircraft is a lot easier for the anti-aircraft gunners to hit, it is also within the range of machine gun and other small arms fire from the ground, and reflects the fact that the Manchester was still struggling.

Fortunately for them Lubeck was not a well defended target, and their luck held. I do not know whether they had been told that would be the case during the mission briefing. 'Remainder of the trip uneventful' just as well, since their ability to throw the aircraft around the sky to avoid any enemy action was still heavily compromised.

On that night nine Manchesters of 61 Squadron took part in the same raid. Ours was not the only crew that had troubles with their aircraft's reliability. Flying Officer Gilpin was in Manchester L7480, immediately after dropping the bombs the aircraft suffered a failure of the hydraulic systems and the engines lost some power. They were forced to land at Binbrook on the way home as their fuel was almost exhausted.

On April 8th they flew to Hamburg in Manchester L7471, again with the same crew to bomb the Blohm & Voss shipyards. The squadron had by now moved to Syerston as part of the preparations to re-equip with the new Lancaster bomber. Syerston had longer, hard surfaced runways and larger reinforced concrete hangars. The six hour trip seems unremarkable in the Operations Record Book, but the statement that they 'bombed concentrated heavy flak' paints a picture of a very fraught time over the target area.

I should explain here what is meant by 'heavy flak'. It does not refer to the amount of anti-aircraft fire, but the calibre of the gun and the weight of the shell. The most common German heavy flak gun at this time was the famous Krupps made Flak 18 usually referred to simply as the 88.

It could fire its 20lb 88mm high explosive round at over 2,500 feet per second to a height of 28,000 feet could fire at a rate of 15-20 rounds per minute. A very formidable weapon.

Medium flak referred to high velocity guns of 20 to 57mm calibre. These fired smaller shells which were not able to reach over about 14,000 feet. They were, however, capable of firing rates of up to 200 rounds per minute and often came in multi barrelled mounts. Any aircraft within their range could expect a thoroughly unpleasant experience.

Light Flak was used to describe anything from small arms, medium and heavy machine guns of 7.6mm to 15mm and the lower velocity 20mm cannons. These presented little danger above about 7,000 feet.

The amount of the anti-aircraft received would be described as low (or small amounts), moderate or intense.

Between the 11th of April and late May 61 Squadron undertook no operational sorties while the crews converted to their newly delivered Lancasters. During this period Sergeants Davies and King were replaced by Oliver Percy Beswick (2nd Wireless operator) and Norman Rhodes Hartley (Mid Upper Gunner), for both men this would be their first operational experience. Beswick was transferred straight from 14 OCU. Hartley had been trained on the Hampden two engine bomber and allocated to 44 Squadron in mid December 1941 just a few weeks before they too began converting to Lancasters so he was immediately sent to 25 OCU to undertake his conversion training and transferred to 61 Squadron directly from there.

**Avro Lancaster in flight.**                    From the Author's collection.

May the 28th was our new crew's first operational flight in a Lancaster. They took R5615 from Syerston to go Gardening off the Denmark coast. Gardening was RAF official slang for marine mine laying. Not usually as dangerous as missions deep over enemy occupied territory. However flying straight

55

and level at a very low altitude over a dark sea on a dark night was still risky and any armed enemy shipping in the vicinity would present a serious challenge. They returned safely after a trip of seven and a half hours.

Their next outing was in Lancaster R5627 on May 30th to Cologne as part of the first 1000 bomber raid and did not to turn out to be such a quiet affair. Again the report does not convey the full extent of their peril. 'Bombs dropped from 8,000 feet while held in a searchlight cone'.

Flying on a straight course at a steady speed while being blinded by the intense lights and with the anti-aircraft gunners having a clear view of the Lancaster illuminated by those multiple searchlights must have made the bomb run extremely uncomfortable and dangerous.

All of the crew would have been staining their eyes to catch any slight clue as to the presence of other aircraft in their vicinity. For them all to then be suddenly subjected to the searingly bright searchlights would have been completely blinding and very disorienting. The pilot would have been unable to read any of the cockpit instruments and would have to fly by feel alone. The bomb aimer would not be able to even see the ground, let alone pick out the target area. I have to assume that he released the bombs immediately, though that is not stated, as it should have been, in the combat report. All of the crew would also have instantly lost their night vision just at the time when they most needed it.

'Searchlights only evaded by flying through smoke clouds over Cologne'. Twisting and turning to find some small scrap of cover from the blinding lights while 999 other bombers were making their straight and level bomb runs through the same patch of sky was a real gamble, there would have been a very high risk of a mid-air collision; but they had no other choice.

'Again caught by flak descended to zero feet, and Sgt Griffiths the tail gunner silenced two gun posts that opened fire on our approach'. Not zero feet, but very low, 200 feet would just about clear any tall buildings or trees, and present only the briefest of targets as they raced past at almost 300 miles per hour.

For our tail gunner to hit the enemy's gun emplacements was very good shooting by anyone's standards. Sergeant Griffiths would have had at the most two seconds to identify the position of the German guns, bring his own Brownings to bear on them and fire before they were out of his range. He managed to do that twice.

A very lucky escape.

# Chapter 14

## Down to Earth with a Bump

A few days later on June 2nd they embarked on their fateful final trip. They took Lancaster R5613 from Syerston and again the target was the Krupps works in Essen. The Operations Record Book simply records that they took off at 00:01 on June 3rd with little cloud cover between the home base and the target area and no more was heard from the aircraft. I did, however, also have the reports that William made to MI9 on his return to Britain.

Straight away I found some discrepancies. All no doubt due to William's rough time between the flight and making the report more than two months later, and the fog of war. According to William the call sign of the aircraft used was QR-L but that was not the one he was in, that was actually QR-B. QR-L was the Lancaster that the crew had flown in on their last, and very memorable, flight to Cologne. He also incorrectly gave the take-off time as 23:45 on the 2nd of June, this was probably the time they started the engines or commenced to queue up for their runway slot and was the actual take off time for the first aircraft from 61 squadron that night.

They arrived over the target on time and at 20,000 feet. The bombs were seen to fall about a mile south of the Krupps works. They were steadily reducing height on the way home and by 02:20 they were near Tirlemont in Belgium and they were down to around 16,000 feet. This was when the pilot spotted a German Messerschmitt Bf110 night fighter flying in the opposite direction about 800 yards to port, and alerted the rest of the crew.

William held his fire in keeping with his training while watching the fighter which was now turning in for an attack from the rear. RAF thinking at the time was that it was taking an unnecessary risk to expose your own position by opening fire too early when the muzzle flashes and tracer rounds would alert not only the fighter that you had seen, but any others in the vicinity. There was still the chance that the enemy might not have had a good view of your aircraft, or may lose sight of it in the dark. But interviews with German night-fighter pilots after the war told a somewhat different story. Even a brief burst of gunfire at extreme range could discourage an attack, the attacker may turn away and try to reposition for another attempt, or seek out another target where the gunner was not so wide awake. Only the boldest pilots would continue the attack.

Nor were the respective weapons in the bomber's favour. Their Browning 0.303s lacked the power and range to do much more damage than just to penetrate the skin of a Bf110 at anything over about 350 yards. The fighter carried a similar set of four machine guns plus two 20mm cannons. These cannons could deliver explosive filled shells at ranges well over 800 yards, just a handful of hits from these could disable a Lancaster.

In this particular attack things were even less in favour of the bomber as the night fighter was now close in line with the moon which was dead astern of the Lancaster, which made it difficult to track. According to Sergeant Griffiths' report he was still watching the German plane when the Lancaster was struck from below and behind by both machine gun and cannon fire. This tore through the rear fuselage working forward to the inner part of the port wing. It is possible that he had actually been watching some reflection or refractions in his Plexiglas turret glazing, but he believed a second fighter had entered the attack unseen and this would appear to be the case.

The Luftwaffe pilot who shot down our crew reported that he approached from astern and below the Lancaster. He did not mention having to turn to make the attack; but neither did he mention another German aircraft. Either way, the Lancaster was now in serious trouble.

The rear turret was completely disabled, William could not turn it as the hydraulic system had been damaged and the guns were stuck pointing downwards. The inner engine and inner fuel tank in the port wing were both already on fire, and that fire was spreading quickly to the rest of the port wing and mid section of the fuselage. William had been slightly wounded in the left arm, but everyone else in the crew reported being unhurt. As the fire was already getting much worse the pilot gave the instruction to abandon the aircraft and bale out.

William had some difficulty in exiting his turret. He was fortunate that the turret was not turned to either side as that would have blocked the doors, and with the damage to the hydraulics preventing the turret from being rotated, he would have been well and truly trapped. The doors and frames had however been deformed in the attack and he could only force them open with the greatest of difficulty. He then had to find his parachute.

It should have been in a cubby box on the side of the aeroplane but had been shaken from there. He finally found it some distance away lying loose on the floor. The crew had already decided prior to the mission that in the event of a bale out the mid upper and rear gunners would use the rear entry door rather than attempt to make the difficult passage to the escape hatches in the forward part of the fuselage. With the now raging fire getting closer all the time, that would in any case have been impossible. When William reached the doorway he found that Hartley had already got the door open and was sitting on the edge.

Leaving the rear door of a Lancaster in flight was not without risk, the safest way was to sit in the doorway and do a sort of forward roll. To stand up and step out meant an almost certain collision with the horizontal tail, to jump out brought a similar risk of collision with the starboard fin and rudder. Either would be very likely to prove fatal. But Hartley was unable to make that final move and drop out of the aircraft.

Griffiths must have realised that this would prevent his escape too, and the only hope for both of them was to take to their parachutes. So he pushed Norman Rhodes Hartley out of the hatch and then proceeded to follow him.

His boots were blown from his feet by the slipstream while he too sat on the edge of the doorway before he had even left the doomed bomber. The rest of the crew appear to have stayed with the Lancaster hoping that the pilot could pull off a survivable crash landing. That, sadly, was not to be. As William descended under the parachute canopy he watched his aircraft crash, totally engulfed in flames, about 4 miles to the north.

I had wondered before why so many aircrew showed significant reluctance to leave a doomed aeroplane and chose instead to make a risky crash landing. In my researches into William's time in Bomber Command I discovered that the parachute training the crews received was not as comprehensive as I had previously imagined. Basically it amounted to little or none. Some squadrons elected to have new crew jump off a high table or platform a couple of times to learn how to fall, but the number of minor injuries this caused usually led to the training being discontinued.

There were no routine practice jumps from aircraft, and crews were therefore not really familiar with any part of the procedure. This may explain Hartley's reluctance to exit the hatch, and the rest of the crew choosing to stay with the aircraft and hoping the pilot could pull off a survivable landing.

Hartley and Griffiths must have realized that the fire in the rear fuselage meant that they simply had to get out. So I can not blame William for shoving his pal out of the hatch. Neither had any chance of survival unless Hartley jumped, and the action could, indeed should, have saved him. The German night fighter pilot reported seeing two open parachutes descending. But it must have weighed heavily on William's mind for the rest of his life. He saw no other parachutes and no sign of Norman Rhodes Hartley has ever been discovered since that night. Only William survived.

61 Squadron sent just five Lancasters to Essen on that night, one other failed to return. E R Seibold was flying Lancaster R5562, and was brought down by flak over the target. Only the navigator W C Howell survived to became a Prisoner of War. Seibold had previously crashed on the 10th of February in Manchester L7478 while at 25 OCU, due to the port engine failing on the approach for landing. The sudden loss of power when travelling so slowly and close to the ground left no time to even attempt to recover the situation. The aircraft was damaged beyond repair. Six of the crew survived, Seibold was injured and the Rear Gunner Frederick

King was killed in the crash.

Seibold had also had reliability problems with his Manchester aircraft R5786 on the night of 5/6th April on a mission to Cologne. Part of the hydraulic system failed, and the bomb bay doors had to be opened manually. The return trip back to base was made with these doors still open. On the night of 1/2nd June he was due to take Manchester L7477 on a mission to Essen, but had to return early with aircraft reliability issues. He probably thought that he was lucky to be flying the much better and more reliable Lancaster on that fateful June night.

William had made seven operational trips in his career thus far in seven different aircraft. (Details of all their operational sorties and a selection of other remarkable flights are given in Appendix II.) Six of those aircraft were lost on operational flights before the end of June 1942. The seventh one, Manchester R5786, was finally written off on the 28th January 1943 after its third crash landing, two caused by reliability issues with the Vulture engines. Neither Bomber Command personnel nor aircraft had ever stood a good chance of surviving to old age. The odds for an airman surviving the war in Bomber Command worked out at less than one in three. That was more than twice as bad as the British and Commonwealth soldiers in the First World War trenches.

Now William was on his way to Belgium by parachute to an uncertain future and unknown fate. He was possibly reviewing his fortune so far, and we will now do the same.

He had been very lucky. Sitting in a very confined turret that had been damaged by machine gun and cannon fire, he had been only very slightly wounded. The turret had been aligned dead astern as he watched the first night fighter, had it been turned to either side then he would have been unable to get out, and although the doors had been damaged this to was not sufficient to prevent him from forcing them open.

He could so easily have been trapped there waiting to be burned alive or killed in the crash. Not a pleasant choice of outcomes. His parachute was loose on the floor of the fuselage. He could have been unable to find it, or it might have been damaged in the attack. Even a small sliver of shrapnel passing through the pack would have damaged the silk canopy, or cut some of the cords. It would not take a great amount of damage to render the parachute dangerously ineffective.

The Lancaster's rear door could have been jammed shut by the Bf110's fire, and the passage forward to the other escape routes was already blocked by the inferno inside the aircraft's fuselage. All in all he had been very lucky to get this far. Granted he had also been very unlucky to have been in a plane subjected to an undetected night fighter attack, and just how unlucky he would never know.

R5613 had been in the first Lancaster to be shot down by a German night fighter. That's bloody bad luck.

When daylight raids had been attempted earlier in the war the casualty rate among Allied bombers had been far too high, and the switch was made to night time operations to reduce the enemy fighters' ability to find and shoot down the bombers. Thereafter most Allied bombers which had been destroyed at night over enemy territory were brought down by anti-aircraft fire, some by problems with the aircraft itself and a few by accidental collisions. German night fighters had shot down some bombers, mostly the older, slower models, but so far not the new Lancaster.

On that fateful night Oberfeldwebel Fritz Schellwat flying a Bf110 which was one of the very few equipped with the newly introduced "Lichtenstein" Airborne Intercept Radar had found our Lancaster and shot it down before any of the crew was even aware that he was there. From then on the advantage would begin to shift towards the intercepting German night fighters.

# Chapter 15

## Where There is a Will There is a Way

13th October          I have shown some of the many techniques and tricks that can be used to sort out from any list of possibilities which are more likely to be interesting, which may be more remote possibilities and even to exclude some as really impossible, and of course, there is always the possibility that the list does not contain the people one wants to find. But with Ann and Elwyn Thomas Griffiths I felt that I was rapidly running out of options, and at this stage could see no promising looking way forward.

With Elwyn Thomas and Ann's marriage having been in 1947 the opportunity to find the family as a unit on the 1939 Register or any of the available censuses simply did not exist. For more recent events finding the family on the electoral rolls can provide some useful leads. Once any children came of age they would be included at the same address, unless they moved out beforehand.

Unfortunately the rolls for the areas in the time period I was interested in were not available to me. The option to travel to North Wales and work through the volumes of un-indexed electoral rolls was certainly not very appealing, but I was beginning to think that was going to have to be the next step.

18th October          While still going over the same ground for the umpteenth time trying to reduce the number of possible Griffiths - Griffiths children in North Wales I just happened to stumble upon a request on one of the Ancestry message boards. A chap there was asking for help, his daughter was going on a school trip to visit some World War

1 sites in France and Belgium, and a part of that was a project to show a connection to someone who had been involved in the war. The child's great-grandfather had served as a soldier in France.

I often respond to these requests, as I see it as an act of remembrance to the soldier concerned. In this case I could see that the responses they had already received were less than helpful, and mindful of the fact that a quick success might just renew my momentum on my own searches, I decided to take a break and see if I could fill in some details for the lass.

In less than a day I had her full family tree back to her Great Great Granddad, one generation earlier than our soldier. I had details of his military service and early discharge, his marriage and children, their marriages and descendants right up to the young girl herself. All from no other information than his name and military service number. That was much more like the timescales I usually manage to work to. William Richard Griffiths was making me look very much like an inept amateur!

25th October         I had checked my e-mail late the previous night and I had one from Gregory, he was passing on a copy of Gwen Harries' will that Di had obtained. I must admit that wills are rarely high on the list things that I check, but when I read this one more thoroughly the following morning it yielded some very useful clues. Indeed it eventually proved to be one of the keys to the whole search.

In the will, which was made a shortly after her husband Aneurin's death, there were lots of points of confirmation that we were on the right track, and some pointers to things that we had missed. There was a bequest to an Anwen Parry, who was identified as Gwen Harries' niece, we had not yet found anything about her; and mention of Gwen's late brother Ellis Parry Davies, the implication of which was that he had died without having any children. She bequeathed her house in Penrhyndeudraeth to Ann and her husband Elwyn Thomas Griffiths making them the main beneficiaries.

Most importantly for our search was the fact that Gwen appointed her niece Ann Griffiths to be one of the executors and also Ann's son Gwynn Morris Griffiths. Interestingly he was referred to in the text as both Griffith and Griffiths. It also gave his then current address in Henllan. This was the very chap we had been looking for since July! Surely now that we know his name and address, we are really going to start make some solid progress.

Even though I now knew his full name, Gwynn's birth record was still proving to be very elusive, so after another wasted day I looked for a different route to track him down, after all we knew that he had been born, so exactly when and where did not matter quite so much and could possibly wait a while. What we had to do was work out how to contact him, and I knew someone who could do that. I sent details to my mystery tree owner.

Checking the address given in the will for Gwynn Morris Griffiths revealed that it had been recently sold, so we would not find him there. There was always the chance that new owner might know his current address. Tracking this fellow down was none too easy, and eventually only led to another dead end. The property had been bought for use as a holiday let, and the previous owner, who was not our man, had not himself owned it for very long. That trail had gone cold.

29th October          The recent electoral rolls for the

North Wales area held several possibilities for Gwynn Morris Griffiths, though the middle name was usually only given as an initial. I did find one that I thought should have been a star candidate in the right area, and soon found a matching telephone number. Since the electoral roll gave me the name of a female family member at the same address I soon found their marriage record. Judging by the date, he was the right sort of age to be our man. By the time I had found this latest lead it was far too late in the day to telephone, that would have to wait until the next morning.

30th October          Another frustrating morning. I made several phone calls to my new prime target, but none were answered. I also made little progress in ruling out any of the other G M Griffiths in the area. Then in the afternoon I did manage to speak to my man, well actually I spoke to his wife. She found the story quite intriguing, but her husband's middle name was Meredith, so he was not the Gwynn Morris that we were looking for. She did not know any members of the Griffiths and Davies families that I had discovered so far, nor did she recognise any of the other names that were of interest in the area. If he was a relative then he was too remotely related to be able to help.

31st October          I did a quick search to see if I could find the Di that had passed Mary Ellen Davies death certificate and Gwen Harries' will on to Greg. I found her on both Ancestry and Facebook. I sent her a message on both sites. I was really only showing off that I could find people quickly; it had taken a mere 20 minutes. She replied to both messages. I thought this to be only a bit of harmless fun; but it would prove to be much more significant later on. I also received a message through Ancestry from Paul a few days later; he too was engaged in the same search.

69

I mentioned the family tree I had found on Ancestry to Di, and asked if she would also message the owner and see if she got a better reception.

2nd November        I managed to find an old copy of the Bona Vacantia list on a backup drive. This lists all of the unclaimed estates from people who have died intestate. Entries are removed either when the estate is claimed or 30 years have elapsed since the original publication. Since William died in 1984 he could have been on this list which was from 2011. He was not mentioned. He had not had anything left in his estate to list.

It occurred to me later in the morning that since his parents' marriage having taken place on the 30th June 1947, Gwynn might well have been born after the beginning of July 1948. That is when the National Health Service started, and meant that his birth would most probably have been in an NHS institution.

There would have been several small maternity units close to Penrhyndeudraeth, but I had found no likely Birth Register Index entries in the area. There was a possibility that if the birth was expected to be difficult, or if any form of emergency arose during Ann's labour, the birth would have occurred in a better equipped main hospital.

I widened my search to all of North Wales, and found just the one entry for a Gwynn M Griffiths born in the Bangor registration district between 1948 and 1970. I hardly dared to think that I had found him. Typically for this search by the time I made my discovery, it was well outside of office hours on a Friday night. I would have to wait to speak to my friendly registrar, and I would have to wait until Monday. I knew that the office would be open on the Saturday, but was likely to be busy, and not a good time to be asking for favours.

3rd November          I found the page of a Facebook group concerned with the history of Penrhyndeudraeth and applied to join. I would be asking for any information about Ann and Elwyn Thomas Griffiths' family there and try to find someone who could pass on a request to Gwynn.

# Chapter 16

## Hot on Gwynn's Trail

4th November 17:06    I had an email from Gregory. From then on he would be including all three of his helpers in any e-mails to help us to co-ordinate our efforts and not spend too much time chasing the same shadows, and suggested that we all did the same. A very good idea. Things were now beginning to hot up as we closed in on William's nephew, and messages would be flying thick and fast from now on.

17:08    I e-mailed Greg and the rest of the team. I had uploaded a family tree to Ancestry with all the details of William Richard Griffiths and his known relatives; I included a link so the other team members would be able to refer to it. I told them that I was close to discovering if the Gwynn Morris Griffiths born in Bangor was our man, and would provide updates as needed.

17:29    The first team e-mail from Gregory. Paul was going to order three marriage certificates for William R Griffiths' in the Liverpool area; he already had one on order from the GRO. He was convinced that there would turn out to be a strong Liverpool connection, but there were a lot of possible marriages in the area.

17:42    An e-mail arrived from Di to the team, mainly as a welcome for me. She added that she had messaged our mystery tree owner on Ancestry, but had no reply so far, nor would either of us ever hear from her.

18:28    Paul e-mailed with details of the parish records for William Richard Griffiths and Ann's baptisms and their parent's wedding. All good confirmation of what we already had established. He had also found the family on the electoral rolls up to 1926. He said that he was unable to find them from 1927 onwards. I replied that Morris had died in April 1926; I had no on-line access to those electoral rolls.

21:31        Di was checking through William's family tree and had noticed that Henry Ifor Griffiths, William's cousin, had been born in Toxteth. Since William died not that far from there she was wondering if this indicated a more general connection of the family to Liverpool.

5th November 11:03    I e-mailed my registrar contact in North Wales. I told her that I had found a possible entry on the indexes for Gwynn Morris Griffiths in Bangor and that I would like to buy the Birth Certificate, but only if the child's mother and father were Ann and Elwyn Thomas Griffiths.

She phoned me back at 15:00. She had checked the records and so the deal was soon done. Gwynn's birth certificate was now on the way to me! But we still had to find out how to contact him.

15:15        I e-mailed the others and told them all that the birth I had found was the right one, and the certificate was on its way by post.

16:51        I picked up an e-mail from Di, she had found a possible Gwynn M Griffiths on the electoral roll in a small village just outside Welshpool, living with his wife Christine M. The address was not far from his last known one in Gwen's will. She could not find a telephone number, and was asking if we thought it was worth sending a letter. I replied that the cost of a stamp was well worth it to find our man, and we knew that he had moved house.

I then checked the record for myself, not that I did not trust her, but I always check other peoples work. It may turn out to be as bad as my own! Or I may pick up some other small nugget of information. As part of that I looked at the on-line maps for the area.

I had a vague idea of the sort of home Gwynn might be able to afford after his inheritance from Gwen, and the sale of the house he was living in at the time. If the place was a small cottage, or a huge mansion, I would have ruled it out.

It was neither, but I did notice that although the village was very small, it had a large pub, which did meals and let out rooms. I telephoned them.

They knew the Gwynn M Griffiths who lived in the village, and told me that when his mother came to visit him they would often all go to the pub for a meal. So his mother could not have been our Ann! Another dead end.

16:59        I emailed Di with the bad news. I had at least saved her the price of a stamp.

19:48        Paul had found a Gwynn M Griffiths listed as a headmaster in the Conway area, and a corresponding address close by, since there was a telephone number on the school's web page he would be ringing them in the morning.

6th November 20:09    Paul had a short conversation with the secretary at the Conway school, and she had requested that he put the whole story into an e-mail to them: he had done that and was waiting for a reply. He had also joined the

Forces Reunited website to try to find anyone who remembered William Richard Griffiths, especially during his posting to RAF Tengah in Singapore. He may just possibly have married there.

20:21        Di had checked for overseas forces marriage records, but had found no likely candidates, but was unsure if the records available to her were complete. She had also found a document listed in the National Archive catalogue for the Air Gunners School where he trained in 1941. This was not available on-line so would have to wait until someone could visit the archive.

20:24        A reply from Paul, he had just contacted a chap who served in Tengah at the same time as William, and had been the base photographer. We may be able to get another image of our man!

7th November 12:13    I e-mailed the rest of the team with a scan of Gwynn's birth certificate which had arrived a little earlier in the post. He had indeed been born in the main National Health Service Hospital in the area, St David's in Bangor.

While I was on-line I received a copy of another electoral roll entry for a Gwynn M Griffiths and his wife in North Wales in an e-mail from Di. With the wife's name being a little uncommon I first checked for their marriage and learned her maiden name. Then when I searched for a Facebook page in her name I was able to pick out her page because among her friends there were several folk who shared her maiden name.

I sent her a message through Facebook and updated the team at 15:34.

15:37        E-mail from Di to the group, she

recalled that this was the same chap she was about to write to when someone in the team had checked with the local pub, and he was not our man.

She was quite right, and it was me that had done that check just two days ago! When I looked back at her e-mails, I saw that I had received the same one twice two days apart, and assumed that they were different. From then on I was to periodically receive multiple copies of many e-mails, and sometimes copies of e-mails I had sent out would arrive in my inbox purporting to have come from one or other of the recipients.

I decided that I was not paranoid; the world really was out to get me!

I did not realize at the time, but this was just the opening salvo in what was to become a real battle. I e-mailed an explanation to the team.

# Chapter 17

## Some Success at Last

8th November 15:31    Paul had found a birth index entry for an Ann Griffiths born 1979 in the same area as Gwynn, and we could have another cousin to trace. She too was on a private tree on Ancestry, and he had messaged the tree owner. I replied that the page number on the index for Ann was a lot higher than Gwynn's, which would lead me to think that it might well have been from a different area within the Bangor Registration District. It was still a possibility though and worth checking out.

17:11          Di replied she also thought that it was possible, but maybe she would have been mentioned in Gwen's will. She had also come across the Old Penrhyndeudraeth Facebook page and had contacted the administrators who were going to post a message on her behalf asking for information.

17:17          My application to join that same Penrhyndeudraeth group was now approved, possibly as a result of Di contacting them on the same topic. I commented on the post that had been made at Di's request asking for help on our behalf, and added a lot more detail.

I also added Anuerin and Gwen Harries to the people that we were interested in, as Aneurin had been a school teacher there and could well be remembered by more people. With nearly 2000 members I thought that we might at last be in with a fighting chance.

9th November 00:57    I had some useful responses to the

post on the Old Penrhyndeudraeth Facebook page through the evening. Much of this merely confirmed what we had already found out. One fellow was sure that his sister knew more details, but could not contact her immediately, another wait. Someone suggested that Gwynn was now living on Anglesey, around the Trearddur Bay area.

Then shortly after midnight I was contacted by an old friend of Gwynn's, this chap had moved to Canada some years previously, but kept an eye on the Old Penrhyndeudraeth Facebook page. He gave me Gwynn's address, and it was in Trearddur Bay. I checked for a telephone number, but could not find one. So I e-mailed the team with the full details, and suggested that it should be Gregory who wrote to him.

10:56        The euphoria comes to a shuddering halt in the face of reality. Di e-mailed a copy of a land registry entry and a property listing from one of the online estate agencies that she had found. Gwynn's house in Trearddur Bay had been sold on the 14th of February the previous year.

It had taken months of hard work to find his address, only to then discover that he had sold up and moved on somewhere else. We still did not know how to contact him or where he was living! This project had thrown up a lot of dead ends and surprises. I had not seen this one coming.

12:43        Paul had found the Estate Agents that had sold Gwynn's house and spoke to them on the telephone. He had asked them if they could pass on his contact details to Gwynn. They did not have his details immediately to hand, but agreed to pass Paul's message on to him later on in the day.

15:33          I was invited on to the Trearddur Bay Facebook page to continue my searches for Gwynn's address, and posted that we had the address of his previous house in Trearddur but needed to contact him. Co-incidentally, Paul e-mailed details of the same Facebook group to the team just one minute later.

16:12          Paul forwarded an e-mail from the Estate Agents. They had spoken to Gwynn and he was happy to have Paul's e-mail forwarded to him. Now if you are expecting this next part you have earned a gold star. The e-mail address they had for Gwynn was incorrect; they would have to wait until Gwynn could sort that out for them. I did not see that one coming either.

22:20          I had several replies to my post on the Trearddur Bay Facebook page, one confirming that Gwynn had been contacted. This would have been the message from his estate agents, as the team still did not have a good address, telephone number or e-mail address for him.

# Chapter 18

## Contact is Established

10th November 14:47  Paul forwarded an e-mail he had received from Gwynn. We have done it. We have found William Richard Griffiths' nephew. The e-mail itself was quite brief, Gwynn had received the message while on the train to London and he would be there for a few days. He would be in touch again once he had returned home. Surely we would soon find out everything we ever wanted to know about his Uncle William's life. If there were any closer relatives, perhaps even news of a wife and children, we would know everything in a day or two. Then his story could be told in its entirety, and his memory preserved.

After such a protracted hard search the next few days would be a long wait.

21:04  Paul e-mailed to provide a link to an article he had arranged to be published in the Liverpool Echo giving the background to our search, some of the details that we had discovered about William's life, and an account of Joséphine Van Durme's time in the Belgian Resistance and with the Comète Line. He hoped that someone in the Liverpool area might have been able to help us with more information about the time he spent there.

22:03  I received a message through Facebook from Gwynn's son asking if we had managed to contact him and offering help if we had not. Having spent four months finding Gwynn, now that we had, it suddenly seemed like everyone else always knew where he was!

15th November 22:08   Paul passed on an e-mail he had just received from Gwynn.

He had been on the train to London when he received the first e-mail from Paul. On the way to see the Armistice Day 1918 - 2018 commemoration at the Cenotaph, so the news was especially poignant to him. He passed on his thanks to the team for all our efforts. He had collected a box of family mementoes from storage, and would be in touch again when he had time to sort through these and found some more information about his uncle William.

16th November 12:26   In reply to Gwynn's thanks I sent him a few family tree charts showing all of his ancestors and cousins that we had discovered. I also said that we owed all that we had done, and much more to the brave lad who had sat of in the tail end of a Lancaster bomber to fight for his country's freedom. They should never be forgotten. I copied the team in on that e-mail.

14:14          I e-mailed my hard working, favourite Registrar. I thanked her for all her help, which, I said, was key to concluding our research. I did not know that we would shortly discover that this was not to be the end of the story, there would be a whole lot more work to do soon!

20:54          Paul copied the team in on an e-mail he had sent to Gwynn He had included the link to the Liverpool Echo article, which outlined the sad circumstances of William's death.

18th November 12:04  Paul forwarded an e-mail which Gwynn had sent to him on the previous evening. Gwynn would be taking a little time to come to terms with the news of his uncle's life and death. He had found it particularly upsetting that he had died alone and in such poor circumstances. He went on to explain that he knew little about his uncle Will; he had met him only once when he himself was just eleven years old, which would have been shortly after William was discharged from the RAF. Gwynn's mother Ann had been brought up by a relative, and had not been involved in William's life. Ann had never answered questions about her early history; it seems that Mary Ellen's remarriage had indeed cast a very long dark shadow.

He had found three photographs of William among his mother's possessions; he described the first as having a note on the back 'My brother Will at 18', a second one was from a studio in Blackpool showing William in his new uniform. He would have been in the area on his first posting to the RAF Mechanical Transport Division and a third showing William with his Air Gunner's wings and sergeant stripes. He had attached those to his e-mail.

Unfortunately these did not get forwarded to the rest of the team. Just how cruel was that. We were all desperate to see what William Richard Griffiths looked like, whether he really was the same man as Gregory's mystery photograph or not, and the gremlins had once again conspired to frustrate us.

15:04    I replied to Paul's e-mail to say that I had not received to photographs of William and asked him to resend them.

I added that I was not totally surprised by the lack of prior contact, and some family 'secrecy'. I thought there were always clues to that in the research. Ann was not with her family on the 1939 register (and we still did not know where she was). It was also a period when remarriage was sometimes viewed as 'not the thing'. There may have been difficulties on the children's part, either with the relationship with their new step-father, or the fact that Mary Ellen remarried. It was even more likely that Mary Ellen perceived these problems to be worse than they actually were.

It really does not take that much for any family to find it has drifted slowly apart.

I also recounted that I was, a few years before, driving along listening to BBC Radio 4. An eminent anthropologist was discussing some of the more remote communities he had visited, I missed the introduction to the article so I could not say where exactly, but one tribe in the Western Pacific had what he described as a unique view of death.

In their culture a man dies three times (they had no particular view as to what happened to women as they did not count for much!). The first time he dies is when he is not around anymore and he could not tell the stories he knew (it was an entirely oral society with no written language). The second time is when the people that knew him stopped telling the stories they had heard from him, and the third and final time is when the people who had never even known him stopped telling the stories that they had heard about him from someone else.

I disagreed with the learned anthropologist, because I believe that we all think along those same lines. Shakespeare is immortal because we still remember him; Beethoven was made immortal by his music. It's exactly the same principle, and it applied to our search too.

We were remembering the William Richard Griffiths that we never even met, but we were having to uncover his life story for ourselves.

15:13        Today the photographs of William turned up. Comparing the fresh faced young lad aged just 19

William Richard Griffiths in early 1942
Courtesy of Gwynn Griffiths

with his new Air Gunners wings and Greg's mystery photo it was indeed the same chap. We had still not yet solved the whole riddle of that other picture, but we now knew it was indeed our William.

17:07        I e-mailed the team; I had finally worked it out who the child living with Gwen and Aneurin Harries on the 1939 Register was.

The entry was, of course blacked out because he or she was born after 1918. Yet we were confident that they had no children. It could surely only be William's sister Ann being brought up by her aunt Gwen. She was the relative that Gwynn had referred to, and Ann had lived there for some time, possibly since not long after her mother's second marriage in 1929.

This would also explain why she was the main beneficiary in her Aunt Gwen's will, and was the reason that our reluctant family tree owner had come to the wrong conclusions. She was not a Nanw Harris, but was an Ann Griffiths known by her pet name Nanw who was brought up by the Harries family.

All of the clues had been there for ages, and I had revisited the problem several times, but it had still taken me two months to figure that simple puzzle out; I obviously still needed more practice at this research lark!

20:09 Paul e-mailed Gwynn and mentioned some of the documents we had uncovered and some of the discoveries we had made detailing William's life and experiences. He asked if Gwynn knew of a wife or any children, as we had so far not been able to find these.

Paul also mentioned his own role in preserving the story of the Comète Line that had been instrumental in returning William to Britain, in particular that the founder of the Comète line, Andrée de Jongh had personally guided William Griffiths from Paris to Spain.

19th November 15:43 Gwynn e-mailed his reply to Paul, which he forwarded to the team at 16:13 the same day. Gwynn had been reading the history of the escape routes over the Pyrenees only a few weeks previously, and was thus familiar with both the Comète Line and Andrée de Jongh. Quite a coincidence.

He mentioned that he had discovered another photograph of William. He described this as showing his uncle Will in his RAF uniform standing with a young woman who was holding a baby at the rear of a terraced house that he was not familiar with. He knew nothing more about the picture. He had not the slightest clue as to the date or place and he certainly did not recognise the woman.

Just to make things a whole lot more difficult, Gwynn was unable to send us a copy of the photograph straight away.

And we were all so desperate to see it as soon as possible. We were in for another long frustrating wait.

# Chapter 19

## William's Escape from Occupied Europe

Since Gwynn had mentioned the Comète Line, now would be a good time for us to look at His Uncle Will's experiences after he was shot down in Belgium.

I had several accounts to draw on. The main two were William's own accounts given to MI9 on his return to England, plus his page from the Evasioncomete web site from the archives of the Comète line. I had in the past read several books dealing with these escape lines, and the Resistance organisations which provided me with further background information. I would need all of these, and more research too.

The MI9 report was particularly frustrating. Even though it was 'TOP SECRET' and subject to very tight distribution limits, for added security it used few names, people in the occupied territories were always referred to very cryptically As examples Jules Colle was referred to as 'a Belgian lieutenant' we will meet him and 'the woman who broke her leg' later on in the story.

There was an appendix that gave all of the names fully cross referenced to the cryptic ones in the report body, but that was on an even tighter distribution list and was always separate from the main report. I have not been able to locate that appendix. To add further confusion, everyone in the Resistance or an escape line used a code name; Josée was Joséphine Van Durme and Andrée de Jongh the founder of the escape line was Dédée to the Comète escape line and 'Postman' to MI9 (she had always called her charges 'parcels'). I will give some of those code names that I know in brackets as the story proceeds, and outline what I have been able to discover of those brave souls that played a part in our story later in Appendix III, which also includes some of their other notable adventures.

From his own account we know that Sergeant Griffiths landed in a field near the road to Brussels close to Plancenoit in the Genappe region at about 02:25 in the morning of the 3rd of June 1942. With a heavy ground mist at the time, he had trouble seeing how far below the ground was and judging how quickly he was rushing towards it. He landed fairly heavily and broke all of his upper front teeth. He had also been shot in his upper left arm. Even though that was not a disabling wound he would still need to get it attended too fairly promptly.

He bypassed the first house he came to, which was about 15 yards from where he landed and knocked at the door of one a little further away. Receiving no reply there he moved on to a third house, from there he was directed to a café. Although he had not yet hidden his parachute or his flying clothing, this was almost exactly the sequence of events that he would have been instructed to perform during the escape and evasion training given to RAF aircrew, and although I did not realise at the time, I already had good evidence that he had received that training earlier in his career.

The photograph with the bloodied shirt fragment that Greg had found was exactly what airmen were advised to provide themselves with during the escape and evasion training, the style of the jacket and tie being quite flamboyantly 'continental' and a decidedly unmilitary hairstyle. The size and even the paper were specified, and two identical copies should be hidden in the airman's working clothing.

When he arrived at the café he met a Belgian man, who I think from the MI9 description of 'a Belgian man trying to get to Britain', would have been Jean Maurice Depraetere (alias Delbo), he crossed into Spain on the night of the 13/14th of June. Fortunately for William, Jean was a former member of the Belgian army, trying to make his way to Britain to continue his fight against the Germans. He was in contact with the Belgian Resistance, and also the Comète escape line.

He provided William with a pair of boots, bandaged his arm and later returned with him to bury the parachute, retrieve his battledress and flying kit, which would later be burnt. This was not without risk. William had landed about 200 yards from a German observation post. They had not seen him land, there was some ground mist at the time, and they may have been distracted watching the Lancaster crashing in flames a few miles away.

This time they would both have had to have been very careful, and lucky, if they were going to be able to bury his parachute and retrieve his flying gear so close to the enemy. But that sort of escapade was not unusual for the local partisans, and their luck held.

From his battledress they also recovered his 'Purse', but the 'Escape/Ration Box' had slipped from his pocket at some stage and had been lost. Both were part of the standard escape kit issued to every airman flying over enemy territory.

The 'Escape/Ration Box' contained enough concentrated food and chocolate to last 48 hours, water purification tablets, matches, fishing line, sewing needle with thread, and a small compass. The 'Purse' had the equivalent of about £12 (roughly a week's wages for a semi-skilled worker) in the currency of the countries that would be over flown and may have to be traversed while escaping, maps, a phrase card in several languages and a magnetised part hacksaw blade, which could be used to both saw small items and also as a compass.

From now on his movements and activities would be controlled by the Comète escape line, and he would need all of their skill and daring to make it back to Britain. For him the price of failure would be to spend the rest of the war in a Prisoner of War camp. For the Belgians the stakes were very much higher. At best they could expect a miserable existence in a prison camp, where their chances of survival would be very low, at worst they would be cruelly and extensively tortured before being executed.

He spent part of this first night at the home of Jules Flament in Genappe, At some time during the day he was moved by Joséphine Van Durme (Josée) to the Berger farm in Plancenoit where Dr Georges Blanpain, who had been brought there by Jules Colle, attended to William's arm, and he then returned to the Flament farm and hid in the hayloft for the rest of the day. The various accounts differ somewhat in the details of how, and where, this meeting took place. Having looked at the timings of them all I believe that to have been the most likely series of events.

Later in the day, probably just after dark, Joséphine and Émile Delbrouck accompanied William in a car to the farm of Gustave Delaide in Roussart near Waterloo. These were the connections that would ultimately lead to this whole story being uncovered.

Joséphine Van Durme was Émile Delbrouck's aunt, and Jules Colle was Joséphine's fiancé. It was when Émile's Great Nephew Gregory was sorting through his Great Aunt Joséphine's effects shortly after her death that the notes she made at the time of the German occupation and the items that were connected to William Griffiths came to light. Gregory was determined from then on to find someone related to William to whom he could tell the whole tale.

Joséphine Van Durme and Jules Colles

William then had to move on as Albert Greindl (Nemo, Desmedt) had been warned by Antoine Goethals that William had been seen by a neighbour who was known by the local Resistance to be a Rexist, a member of a right wing political party sympathetic to the Nazi cause, many of whom were active collaborators. Gustave Delaide drove him in his car part of the way to Waterloo where they were met by Joséphine and Jules. So by the night of the 5th of June William was at 288 Chaussée de Bruxelles in Waterloo, being sheltered by Joséphine Van Durme and her mother Jeanne Plettinckx.

91

On the 6th of June, again probably late in the evening, William was on the road again. This time he was going to the home of Octave Mondo and Suzanne Watrin at 56 Guillaume Stocqstraat in the Ixelles area of Brussels, where he would stay for the next six days. William, and several other sources, stated that he travelled on the rear of a tandem accompanied by a gendarme, but the daughter of the house has reported that he had been brought there by Dr Goethals.

There are several ways that these accounts can be reconciled. Dr Goethals may have been on the front of the tandem, or may have arranged the move and been there to meet the pair. I think that the latter may be the more likely, as he could then ride back to Waterloo. The tandem riding gendarme turns up a few times in the stories from both the Comète Line and the Belgian resistance from that time, but so far he remains another brave patriot for whom I have no name.

On the 11th or 12th of June William was taken by Marguerite Van Lier (Alias Michèle, Melle Mitchell, or Peggy) probably by tram, it's about seven kilometres, to the home of Carl Servais and his wife at 28-30 Stevens Delannoystraat in the Laeken district. Carl was the radio operator for the local Resistance. Benjamin Goldsmith, the rear gunner of a Stirling bomber who had been shot down on the night of 5/6th June near Pietrebais, was already staying there. There are brief descriptions of the adventures all of the allied personnel that William met during his trip to Spain in Appendix IV.

Marguerite Van Lier collected the two men on the 23rd of June and took them to the main railway station, again most probably by tram, where they met Georges D'Outremont with two more evaders, Reginald John Collins and Marian Henryk Zawodny. Collins was an Australian Bomb Aimer/Front

Gunner in a Wellington bomber taking part in the 1,000 bomber raid on Cologne during the night of 30/31st May. Zawodny was a Polish Gunner in a Wellington bomber which was shot down just after midnight on the morning of the 11th of April.

The two Belgian guides bought tickets for Valenciennes just over the French border on the Paris line; they would all be travelling in a reserved first class compartment. While on the train they would purchase supplementary tickets to Paris. This was a simple but effective ruse to avoid too close inspection of Identity Cards and travel documents at the station, since passengers with direct tickets from Brussels to Paris would often arouse the authorities' suspicions.

This part of the trip to the southeast corner of France had already undergone several refinements since the first one in 1940, and this was to be the sixteenth such journey. Initially they would take the train to Quievrain, cross the border into France on foot, and then take another train or tram to La Corbie, a village near Amiens. As many locals crossed the border this way to go to work, to trade or see family, it did not appear too suspicious.

Then they had to cross the river Somme using a small boat during the night, although on the first trip the boat could not be used as there were a small party of people too close to its hiding place. The group, 11 in all, were obliged to find a new spot and swim the river as quietly as possible. This was aided by a rope that they had obtained and slung across the river and an inflated tractor tyre. It was still very hard work for the group leader, and founder of the Comète line, Andrée De Jongh (code named Dédée) who accompanied each of the non-swimmers across. It took over an hour, and even in July the river ran very cold.

This determined, resolute and resourceful young woman would time and time again be called upon to prove how tough a person can be in pursuit of a just and worthy cause. She was a legend in her lifetime, and remains one to this day. Hundreds owed their lives and liberty to her, for which she paid a very heavy price.

Our party were met at the Gare du Nord station in Paris by Frédéric De Jongh (Paul) who was Dédée's father, and René Coache. Collins and Goldsmith went to the home of René and his wife Raymonde at 71 Rue de Nanterre in Asnières-sur-Seine while Griffiths and Zawodny were guided by Frédéric to 2 Rue Emile Dequen in Vincennes, the home of Léon Violette and Béatrice Crane. A few days later two soldiers from the Argyll & Sutherland Highlanders arrived at Rue Emile, James (always known as 'Jimmie') Goldie and William MacFarlane. On the 21st of March 1942 they had escaped from Stalag IXc at Bad Sulza in Germany where they had been used as forced labourers.

On the 30th of June Zawodny and Griffiths were taken to the Château de Vincennes  6 Avenue des Érables in Saint-Maur-des-Fossés, where they met Bernard (Bunny) Evans, William McFarlane was also there. This was the main 'office' of the Comète Line in Paris and would see many comings and goings of both evaders and Comète Line helpers. Evans had been the rear gunner on a Wellington bomber shot down near Montigny-le-Tilleul in Hainaut on a mission to Cologne on the night of 30/31st March. Both Zawodny and Evans would have to wait for the next trip over the Pyrenees as their forged ID papers were not ready.

On July 4th, Andree De Jongh and Elvire Morelle escorted

Griffiths, Goldsmith, Collins and Waclaw Czekalski to the Gare d'Austerlitz. Waclaw Czekalski (his given name is sometimes reported as Waclan) was a Polish Pilot serving with the RAF who had been shot down in a Wellington bomber on the night of 5/6th of May. From Paris they would be travelling to Saint-Jean-de-Luz which is south of Biarritz on the Bay of Biscay and close to the Spanish border. Again they would use a reserved first class compartment. When the train stopped at Bayonne three more Comète Line workers boarded the train and joined the group, Albert Johnson (Bee or B) and two young women. I have not been able to identify either of these two brave ladies for certain, but this was a task often undertaken by Elvire De Greef (Tante Go) and her daughter Janine.

On arrival at Saint-Jean-de-Luz station at around 9:00 Collins and Czekalski were guided out through the main exit while Griffiths and Goldsmith were shown out through the rear door of a toilet block for which the escape line had obtained a spare key. This simple ploy shows us another subtlety used to avoid detection. The group was split as four young men travelling together would stand out more than two men and a young woman. Initially the second half of the party would have had to climb out through the lavatory window, but that would, in itself, have aroused suspicions had it been observed. So it was worth the effort to obtain a key and have a copy made.

Elvire Morelle immediately returned to Paris, she would not be attempting the crossing since she had broken her leg on a previous journey, and we will come to that a little later. The rest of the party would spend the day and the next night in the flat of Ambrosio San Vincente and Maritxu Anatol at 7 Rue Salagoïty in Saint-Jean-de-Luz, where William left a thank you note in the visitor's book. In the interest of security this note was written in Welsh.

On the morning of the 7th of July the party moved on to Urrugne, sometimes this trip was made on foot and at other times using borrowed bicycles, always avoiding the main road and using the narrow lanes instead. They arrived at Maison Thomás-Enea, the farm of Dominique Irastorza and his wife Françoise Halzuet otherwise known as Frantxiska, where they would spend the day.

In the evening the party set off to cross the border. There are again discrepancies in the various reports, all four airmen were certainly in the group, and there is general agreement that there were two Basque guides, and at the time these were most likely to have been Florentino Goikoetxea and Donato Errazti (or possibly Tomás Anabitarte). While some accounts say that both Dédée and Albert Johnson (Bee) crossed with them, William reports that it was Andrée De Jongh, but the Comète Line records that it was Albert Johnson; it was usual for two Comète Line members to accompany the evaders over the border.

I have not been able to find this particular crossing itself recorded in any detail anywhere, but at the time one of the usual routes would have been south to Mount Calvarie using narrow tracks and then on to the farm at Pitara. Turning west they would pick up the valley of the Lantzetta Erreka stream and follow that to emerge on the banks of the Bidassoa River which formed the border with Spain, opposite the old San Miguel station. There was a footbridge there, but the old station building was used as a border crossing guard post by the Spanish.

If the guards were vigilant the party could divert a few

hundred yards up the river and attempt the crossing there. The water was not too deep, but it always ran fast and cold. This crossing point is now used for white water canoeing. If the Bidassoa was in spate, and it often was, then a longer diversion would be required adding around four hours to the journey. Usually though the guards were not too assiduous in performing their duties and it was possible to sneak past while they were warming themselves inside the building.

Florentino was in the habit of arriving there just a short while before the guards were changed late at night, if the guards were outside and on watch when the party arrived they would simply wait awhile to see if the next crew were less attentive. This cunningly simple strategy often paid off.

Of course all of that was subject to change at very short notice if patrols were encountered on either side of the border, both of which happened all too frequently, including on the very next crossing. Sometimes too the weather turned really nasty as it often can in the mountains. Trips sometimes had to be aborted.

Once over the border there was another steep climb through the forest to the heights overlooking the old fort at Pagogaña, though this could not be seen through the dense woodland. Now there was an easier descent into the valley below which went north towards Irun, the escape route however continued to the west. There were a few more wooded ridges to cross before reaching the small villages around the Elizalde, Gerutze and Arrague area where they could recover from their exertions in one of the safe houses there.

On some routes the party could occasionally catch a glimpse through the trees of San Sebastian on the coast to the north-west. The sight of a seaside town lit up by just a few meagre streetlights must have been both surreal and somewhat unsettling after years of strict blackout.

We know that our party arrived safely, though we don't know exactly where. 'A village' is all that is in the records. The Basque and Comète Line guides would have immediately returned to Urrugne. The 'parcels' would rest for a while and then be taken by Bernardo Aracama in his taxi to San Sebastian.

Our particular party then travelled on to Vittoria Gastiez, the capital of the Basque region. They were picked up in a car from there by the Assistant Military Attaché from the British Embassy in Madrid and taken to Gibraltar on the 9th of July. They remained there until the 21st of the month when they sailed to Gourock in Scotland, arriving there on the 30th.

# Chapter 20

## A Not so Quiet Walk in the Hills

The fact that William Richard Griffiths managed to pass so uneventfully from his initial landing outside Plancenoit all the way back to Britain in no way means that that had been an easy task with little danger involved. Quite the opposite, our William had again been very lucky. Many others did not fare so well. That the Comète Line helped 287 allied servicemen and 76 other persons escape to Britain stands as a testament to all of the people involved. In addition 389 allied airmen were sheltered until the liberation, some individually or in small groups in safe houses, and others in the 'Marathon' camps set up in remote forests.

Only two escapers died while under the protection of the line although unfortunately 237 were captured by the German forces. More than 150 Comète Line members paid the ultimate price for their service and countless others endured unimaginable horrors in the Nazi prison camps until they were liberated. Though sadly some of those died soon afterwards as a direct result of their harsh treatment.

The crossing of the Spanish border was never without risk. Although the northern foothills of the Pyrenees are not very high, around 2,000 feet or so, they are not gentle rolling hills, but often very steep and rocky. Added to which the guides were obliged to use the narrowest sheep or goat tracks in the deeper boulder strewn valleys and across the sheerest slopes to minimise the risk of running into any border patrols. To complete the trip at night, and often in foul weather, was no easy feat.

The key to a successful crossing lay mostly in the knowledge, daring and determination of the Basque guides. These were all seasoned 'mountain men' and almost all of them made a large portion of their usual income from smuggling. A dangerous game even in peacetime. Florentino Goikoetxea, who we have just met, came to be regarded as the best of the lot and was awarded the King's Medal by the British and the Legion d'Honneur by the French after the war. (Incidentally, when being presented with his medal by King George VI, in answer to his question "And what do you do?" this largely uneducated man who only ever spoke Basque managed to reply "I am in import export.")

As well as the terrain and weather the mountains held other perils. The French side was patrolled by both civil Gendarmes and the German Military, and on the Spanish side the Carabiñeros were very active. Meeting any of these could be very bad news.

 In February 1942 (MI9 has the date of the 6th, but the Comète Line records show it as the 9th). Elvire Morelle had accompanied Florentino Goikoetxea and Dédée in order to learn the route, and they had safely delivered their 'parcels'. Some accounts of this incident report that the Basque guide was Manuel Iturrioz, including some of the Comète Line records, and in the  Comète Line chronology Florentino only took over guide duties when Manuel was arrested on 19th of April 1942 (he escaped shortly afterwards, but then had to go into hiding).

On the return trip over the mountains in the pitch dark and in a blustery snow shower Elvirie missed her footing, slipped and broke her leg very badly. The two girls had to wait in silence without shelter in the icy wind, rain and sleet while

100

the Basque guide borrowed a mule from one of the nearby farms. Whether he asked first, or considered it too rude to awaken the owner in the small hours just before dawn is not clear.

He rejoined the pair shortly after dawn, Dédée and the guide managed to get Elvire onto the mule, unfortunately not without causing her even more pain, and he led them back down the mountains to an isolated, empty hut. There the party waited for nightfall. Only then could they resume their uncomfortable journey back to Rentería on the Spanish side of the border. The guide and Elvire were driven by Bernardo Aracama to an unnamed Basque doctor, who did a very fine job on the broken leg. It is a tribute to the good doctor's skill and discretion that Elvire was able to make a full recovery in peace. In the cryptic code of MI9 documents 'the woman who broke her leg' would always serve as her unique identifier.

On July 26th 1944 Florentino made his last trip across the border to deliver and pick up messages. Since the D-Day invasion there had been far fewer servicemen repatriated by the escape lines, but he continued to act as international postman for the Comète Line and, as in this instance, the French Résistance.

On his return trip he was intercepted by a German patrol and shot four times. Even with a badly broken leg and shattered kneecap his contrived to hide the documents he was delivering. He was then taken under guard to the hospital in Bayonne. Elvire de Greef (Tante Go) visited him there the following morning. Actually she visited the rather bemused patient in the adjoining bed whom she had never met before. As she rose to leave she dropped her bag. When she stooped to pick it up she slipped a piece of paper under the sheet on

Florentino's bed.

Neither had exchanged so much as a glance nor acknowledged the others presence, but Florentino had well and truly got the message! The two German guards had not noticed a thing.

Later that same day Fernand De Greef, who was wearing a Gestapo Officer's uniform, and two gendarmes working with the resistance in white coats posing as stretcher bearers showed up at the hospital in a 'borrowed' ambulance. Fernand produced all the papers authorising them to remove Florentino. He was driven away and remained in hiding until the Nazis abandoned south-western France the following month.

P02603.00

A picture of Florentino with some of his comrades after his leg had been set and plastered following his rescue.

Of course there were many other encounters with the local border guards. On the 19th of July 1942, which was the very next trip over the mountains after our William's escape, Manuel Iturrioz and Tomás Anabitarte were guiding a party, with Donato Errazti going ahead to check that the trail was safe. The Comète Line leader was Andrée De Jongh, the evaders were Marian Henryk Zawodny, Bernard "Bunny" Evans, both of whom we have already met with John Henry Watson and Joseph A Bruneau Angers, 2nd pilot and rear gunner respectively in the same Vickers Wellington which had been shot down by flak on the night of June 16/17th 1942 during a mission over Essen.

Before they had reached the river they were confronted by two gendarmes, who shouted out at them to halt. Evans immediately jumped behind a nearby bush and hid, Zawodny, who was the last in the line, bolted back the way they had come and the rest of the party scattered. Except for John Watson.

He had either tackled, or been caught by, one of the gendarmes and was scuffling with him when a shot was fired, possibly accidentally. From Watson's somewhat colourful language the policemen soon realised that he was English (he was actually Canadian) and instantly the whole situation changed. The gendarmes became very friendly!

The three talked for a while about what to do next and then they made their way to the Police Station at Béhobie, taking great care to avoid a German patrol that they almost bumped into on the way.

At the Gendarmerie the two policemen convinced the officer in charge of the station to shelter Watson, and he spent a fairly comfortable night in a cell. Later the next day one of the Comète Line helpers, Maritxu Anatol, probably sent by Tante Go, visited the police station on some pretext and reported back that Watson had not been arrested, but was being well looked after and was not locked up.

That evening the policemen produced a large, detailed map. They showed Watson how to get to a crossing point close by where he would be able to swim the Bidassoa, and how to avoid the areas patrolled by both the German and Spanish border guards. He managed to cross the river undetected, but at some point after that he must have taken a wrong turn and was picked up by the Carabiñeros.

While several evaders were helped by friendly gendarmes in both France and Belgium, in Spain the outlook was much more bleak. Although officially a neutral country Spain was much more closely aligned with the Germans, their forces having helped the Spanish fascists win the recent civil war.

Many members of the Spanish Police, at all levels, were actively collaborating with the Gestapo which had agents in almost all of the police stations in the border regions. In Basque country this often put the Carabiñeros at odds with many of the local population and relations were often both strained and tense. If they had followed the Geneva Convention Watson should have been questioned, and if his story that he was an escaping prisoner of war held up, then he should have been turned over to the British Embassy without delay.

All evaders were 'encouraged' by the escape and evasion training and the Escape lines to have a story ready that they had been, at some stage, captured by the German or French authorities and either escaped or been released, this would be enough for them to be considered as escaping Prisoners of War and not evaders. Even modest embroidery of an ID check, or railway ticket check that resulted in a brief detention should have been sufficient. Evaders could be interned for the duration, while escaping POWs should have been turned over to the care of their embassy and repatriated to their home land.

Watson's story follows a slightly different track. This was not at all unusual for allied personnel caught in Spain. He was interrogated, roughly and at some length, by a man in civilian clothes. Who, and what his title was, is not known but many similar interviews were known to have been conducted by Gestapo officers, often posing as something less sinister.

On the 29th of August he was transferred to the notorious Miranda de Ebro prison camp. Conditions, and particularly the food, there were appalling. He was not released to the care of the embassy until September 30th, and finally arrived back in Britain on October 15th.

The rest of the party retried the trip on the 20th, without Watson of course, and crossed successfully to Oyarzun. They were picked up from there by car and after spending a few days in Madrid they crossed into Gibraltar in an ambulance.

On the 23/24th December 1943 a group of evaders was involved in a crossing of the Bidassoa that shows just how treacherous the journey could be. The party was led by Basque guides Manual Olaizola (otherwise known as Cestona) and Martin Errazkin, with several Comète Line members Jean-François Nothomb (Franco), Albert Ancia (Daniel Mouton) and Count Antoine Alja d'Ursel (Jacques Cartier).

The evaders were all USAAF personnel, pilot James Frederick Burch, Lloyd Albert Stanford a bomb aimer, both from the same B17 shot down on a mission to Münster, pilot

Robert Zeno Grimes whose B17 was shot down in Belgium before reaching his target and Arthur James Horning who had been to co-pilot of a B17 shot down over Holland, and Roland Bru (Robert Pasdurand). Bru was acting as an international postman between British Intelligence and the Resistance. d'Ursel was escaping to Britain as he was thought to be in imminent danger of arrest.

When the party reached the river it was running high and fast, and at that time of year very cold indeed. The guides decided that a crossing was still possible, and the men took off their trousers which they would then carry tied round their necks. With the freezing cold water up to their chests and the swift current Grimes lost his footing and was only saved by hanging on to another evader.

As one of the guides was helping d'Ursel, who would be the last man across, into the water there was a burst of gunfire and d'Ursel lost his grip on the guide and was swept away. James Burch also apparently slipped while attempting to climb out of the river on the Spanish bank and was also carried away by the current; all of the rest of the party were by then ashore on the Spanish side.

Nothomb started to search downstream and when he received an answer to his calls he recrossed the river and found d'Ursel. After some discussion they again attempted the crossing, but as soon as they were in the water there were more shots fired. d'Ursel was once again carried away by the swift current. This time Nothomb could not find his friend and had to remain on the French side of the river.

Ancia, Bru and the three remaining American airmen were taken prisoner by the Carabiñeros. The bodies of Burch and d'Ursel were recovered by the Germans the following day.

Their burial place is not known, but a monument to the two men now stands near the crossing point.

# Chapter 21

## The Search Recommences

Gwynn's mention of his photograph of William with a young woman and babe-in-arms had come as a surprise to the whole team, no, much more than a surprise, it was a bombshell. Did we finally have evidence that our man had married? And had a child? When? Where? The only thing that was now certain was that there would be a whole lot more work to do. Since neither Gwynn nor his mother Ann had been involved in William's life sadly we would not be picking up much more information from him. Our cheerful assumption that he would simply tell us all we ever wanted to know had vanished.

We were left with no option but to start again with what we had, which did not amount to very much. We did not at that time even have the photograph to study.

We had the long, far too long, list of possible marriages for a William R Griffiths. We would have to find a new way to reduce the number of possibilities there. We needed a much better idea of where and when he may have married, and where he was living when the baby was born. There were his service records, but so far we had not found them to be of much help, none of us really knew how to interpret some of the more cryptic entries. Plus all the useful personal data was blanked out. There were, I now know, subtle hints there, but we would not spot them for a long while. We needed more clear, straightforward no nonsense information.

19th November 16:19  Di e-mailed the team. She found it fascinating that Gwynn had such a recent connection to the Comet Line story and was, of course, keen to see the new picture. There followed some more e-mail exchanges about the mystery photograph and what we might have been able to deduce from it.

18:28        Greg had found a picture on the internet of Sergeant Pilot Stanley Holmes Lincoln who had been the 2nd pilot for William's crew; it showed six of the crew standing together before a flight. The seventh crew member had, presumably, taken the photograph. The two pilots were in their uniforms and the others in their bulky flying gear, he was sure one of the heavily garbed airmen was indeed William.

19:33        Paul e-mailed that he would be searching for the crash site of the Lancaster, using the MI9 reports and maps to determine the rough location and then on the ground to find any remaining evidence. The occupying German forces had recovered and buried the bodies and salvaged the wreckage at the time, but we had found no exact location recorded.

I had another long look at William's service record. I was trying to piece together where he was, and when, following his return to Britain. It was not an easy task, much of the handwriting was difficult to read, and some had faded badly. The abbreviations were often mystifying, and not all could be resolved. There were several periods of foreign posting too.

So after a couple of days there were still more questions than answers. Nor was I confident that finding where he was stationed would necessarily pin down the place of any possible marriage.

He would have been meeting a lot of eligible young ladies from all over Britain during his wartime service. Many of them could well have been in the WAAF. If he had married one of these the marriage could have taken place close to her station, which may not have been same one as where they met, or even back at her usual home town. That could be anywhere. Without at least a clue as to roughly when and where, we could not hold out much hope of ever finding a marriage.

20th November 15:22  I realized that as William had escaped his burning aeroplane by parachute he would have been eligible to join the exclusive Caterpillar Club. I had many years ago read a book 'Into the Silk' about the Caterpillar Club and detailing many instances of where parachutes had saved lives. This was open only to airmen whose lives had been saved by using an Irvin parachute. The club is still administered by the same company, now called IrvinGQ. The badge was a gold silk moth caterpillar with red eyes.

I sent them an e-mail asking if they had any information that could help us and outlined the circumstances of Williams escape, and why we were trying to find any living relatives. A long shot as not everyone who is eligible either knows about or bothers to join this club.

21st November 20:15  Paul  forwarded  another  E-mail exchange between him and Gwynn. As well as repeating his thanks, Gwynn said that he was taking some time to both absorb and come to terms with what he had so recently learned. He would be going through his box of family mementoes and would be passing on to us anything that might help along with the new mystery photograph.

We were all so desperate to see that picture. I don't think that I was the only one who felt that it would hold the key to achieving what we had worked so long and hard for. And it did prove to hold that key, but it would still turn out to be a harder puzzle to solve than any of us anticipated.

21:59          We all received an e-mail from Greg. In this instance I will quote most of it here exactly as he sent it:-

*"Imagine if somehow Gwynn will find new relatives! Hopes up !*

*Let me take a moment to say thanks, before I forget to do this!*

*PS: Just as Gwynn, I would also come to meet you in person to come and thank you personally for all the effort and help you have given me.*

*I could NOT have done this one my own!*

*After 6 months we got our breakthrough and this investigation has brought me from Belgium to the UK and to Germany and I have met amazing people. Amongst them is this team of four! It started when I stumbled upon Williams possessions that I, at first, had no clue what it was.*

*That's when it all started. Not only was I busy sorting out the story of William but also the story of Josephine van Durme, her Resistance members, the plane-crash, her prison time, visiting the camps in Belgium and East Germany, becoming a part of the Cometline family, learning about the Belgian resistance movement, reading A LOT of books, The list of people that have helped me along the way goes on... Not only am I proud of what we achieved but this gives my heart so much warmth to see how we, strangers at first, worked together to try and solve this amazing quest. Miracles do Exist !*

*There is no way I can think of to repay you and to thank you for your hard work and research. I will repeat myself by saying that I could NOT have done this without you: Rob, Di and Paul!*

*My upmost and sincere eternal gratitude and respect. If there's anything I can do for you, do not hesitate to ask!*

*I will visit you al, or we arrange a meet up either in Brussels or the UKl and have our celebration and this to honour, not only William, but all the Allied airmen who gave their lives so that we could live in freedom.*

*I am sure this story of William and the Comet line deserves a place in history. and it will !*

*Gregory Delbrouck, who is enjoying the world famous Westmalle Tripel !"*

I could not have agreed more, and raised my own glass to William, the Comète Line, Gregory and the team that evening. We had certainly done well, but the game was not yet over, so we could not sit back and rest on our laurels. There was still a lot more work to do before this project would be concluded.

I replied and said that his thanks were not necessary we had done it all in honour of a forgotten hero who should be remembered for his service, a sentiment echoed by the rest of the team.

22nd November 14:58  I received a reply from the Caterpillar Club. As well as a leaflet explaining the club's purpose, and how to apply for membership they had also sent a scan of Sergeant Griffiths' original application letter. He had written on headed paper from the Sergeants' Mess at RAF Penrhos on the 19th of August 1944. I checked his Service Record as saw that he was an Air Gunnery Instructor there at the time. I copied this information to the rest of the team.

Gunnery School RAF Penrhos                                    © IWM (CH 574)

I then did a search of the marriages between 1942 and 1948 in Caernarvonshire, Penrhos would have been under the Pwllheli registration district and there were two possibilities there, with another one in the adjoining Caernarvon district that would have included the village of Llandwrog. There was an airfield there that was also used by the Penrhos Air Gunnery School.

It looked like I had at last found some good leads to the marriage I had been chasing for such a long time. Unusually I had made the discovery during office hours, so I telephoned the Register Office straight away. I asked them to check the entries and if the groom's middle name was Richard (the middle name is not listed on the index, just an initial) and that his father was a Morris Griffiths I would buy that certificate. I was told that neither condition was met on any of the three. We had still not yet found our man.

As I am writing this, and since I need to make sure that I get the timeline right, I am also checking through the e-mails sent between the team members at the time. I can now see that I did not update them on this particular set back. It must have affected me more than I realised at the time, and from now on I notice a marked reluctance on my part to search for William's marriage without a much firmer idea as to where and when that may have taken place. We did have some clues, but neither I nor anyone else in the team realised that at the time.

Instead I once again started to review everything we knew, and everything we had discounted, to see what had been missed, misinterpreted or wrongly discarded. Apart from responding the other team member's e-mails I was to spend the next two weeks solely on this boring task. And I found nothing of any significance.

16:26        Paul had found a possible marriage in Crosby from 1961. I replied that I thought it very unlikely that it would be our man, as he was serving in the Far East in 1961. A pity as this William R Griffiths had married a woman called Sylvia, and researching her would have been relatively easy.

16:46        Greg had compared the handwriting on William's application to the Caterpillar Club and his letter to Joséphine Van Durme that he sent after his escape back to Britain. He thought that they were certainly written by the same person.

23rd November 11:24   Di had found a probate record for an Ellen Arlanwen Owen Griffiths who died in 1966 aged 47, and the probate was administered by her husband William Richard Griffiths who was a farmer. The marriage had taken place in 1944 in Pwllheli. I replied that William was not known to have been a farmer, his father had been, but he died when William was only five and he had been a grocery shop assistant on the 1939 register and still was when he joined the RAF in 1940.

I reminded both DI and Paul that the GRO, and the local Register Offices, would check the groom's father's name if requested, so they need not buy too many wrong certificates.

12:24          Paul said that he had joined the Liverpool and South West Lancashire Family History Society and posted a request for information on their forum.

14:42          Di had a message from a member of the Liverpool FHS forum from someone who had seen her family tree for William Richard Griffiths on Ancestry bringing Paul's message to her attention and suggesting that they could help each other!

17:11          Paul had received a suggestion that the records held by Fazakerely NHS Trust could help. He thought it a good call, William was only 63 when he died and had been discharged from the RAF as being 'physically unfit' so may have been a frequent patient there. In the end he discovered that they only held the records up to 1944.

25th November 16:17   Paul was going to contact the Royal Air Force Association to see if William had ever been a member. They might have been able to help us track his whereabouts after his discharge in 1962.

27th November 19:43   Paul had found 3 different William R Griffiths on the Electoral Rolls in the Liverpool area, and wanted to know if they had been checked out. Since the spouses were also listed the marriages should have been easy to find.

My reply was less than helpful; I just thought that there were simply too many possible marriages in the Liverpool area to go chasing after each one. I needed a good reason why any particular marriage was any more likely than all of the others.

I can see that I was finding it very hard to be positive at this stage. I left it to Paul to check for the dates of the possible marriages.

28th November 15:27   Paul had recruited a new member to the team, John. They had met during a recent Comète Line weekend, and he was an experienced genealogy researcher. We all welcomed him aboard.

This could hardly have come at a better time for me. I was glad to have a fresh pair of eyes reviewing all the mistakes that we had inevitably made (otherwise we would have been home and dry ages ago!).

3rd December 12:14   John's first e-mail to the team. He had reviewed all the information that Paul had provided to him and had some questions on the death certificate. There was no middle name there, just William Griffiths and his occupation was given as Airman. As well as the missing Richard he would have expected to see a more recent occupation, and Airman did not necessarily prove an RAF connection. The place of birth was also given as Liverpool. Although the birth date was absolutely accurate, William Griffiths was a very common name.

He had raised a valid point, and was querying exactly the sort of early assumption where we might have led ourselves astray.

I rechecked the births for the first quarter of 1921. There were three William Griffiths listed, two of whom were born in Lancashire. There were a further 18 William Griffiths who had a middle name, but which may not have appeared on any death certificate, from these three had been born in Lancashire. None of the 21 possibilities had actually been born in Liverpool.

12:48          Paul replied that the Field Lane Centre, the hostel he had been living in immediately prior to his going into hospital, had made a newspaper appeal for any family members or other friends of William's to get in touch with them at the time of his death. They obviously had little information about him.

13:50          Paul had also checked and found no William R Griffiths had been born in the Liverpool area in 1921.

13:52          I replied that in my opinion the chances of any of the other candidates having the same birth date and a previous occupation as an Airman meant we had the right man. Death certificates often throw up anomalies, after all the only person who knows all the answers is no longer in a position to fill the form out.

The wrong place of birth did not strike me as significant at all. Jill Duffy, the person who provided the details would have known his date of birth from his medical records, and probably his last occupation, but not necessarily his place of birth. Since he had died of Bronchopneumonia and Cancer of the throat his Welsh accent, and I suspected that he may well have still had a slight one, may not have been obvious. All in all I was still convinced that we had the right chap.

I had my own theory as to why he did not appear to have had a new occupation after leaving the RAF. After 22 years he may have been to some extent institutionalised, and would have been comfortable with living in a hostel. I also thought that would enable him to spend his modest RAF pension a little unwisely, but I would keep that suspicion to myself for the time being.

13:54        I received another e-mail from John. He had found a very likely looking marriage for our William, back near his home town just after the war. He had the lady's birth date and where she was living from the 1939 Register and three probable children. All very promising, except that it was Katie Hughes again. I replied straight away that she had already been checked out with both her daughter-in-law and our helpful Registrar.

17:36        I already had a basic family tree for William, which I now tidied up, adding some corrections and giving proper references as to where the evidence had been sourced.

I e-mailed the rest of the team offering copies in various formats since the Family Tree software that I still use was always a rare beast and they were unlikely to have that. I also reminded them of the link to the on-line tree on the Ancestry site, which I was going to update too. I reasoned that John would more easily be able to sort out what we had already ruled in or out.

4th December 14:55    John had discovered that William had joined the Royal Air Force Escaping Society, and would be asking them for information, he would also be checking to see if he had also joined the Air Gunners Association.

9th December 10:28    I picked up another e-mail from Paul. He said that he would have expected William to have settled down reasonably comfortably on his RAF pension into an entirely conventional middle class life. He also thought that the blanked out family sections on his RAF record meant that he must have had a wife and children, otherwise those sections would not have needed to be obscured. He felt that it was odd that he had simply fallen off the radar.

10:54    I replied to Pauls e-mail, and this is another one that deserves to be quoted.

*"The relevant sections of WRG's service record would be blanked out, even if they were already blank. Part of the 'if it moves, salute it etc.' mentality I guess. You can sometimes get a wee clue from text that almost escapes the box, but only to confirm that there is something hidden away."*

I just wish now I had taken some notice of what I had written! Had I actually checked the service record at the time we might just have saved a month's hard work.

10:55    Another e-mail from Paul. He had found a marriage to a Rose Hall in the North Liverpool district in late 1946. He reasoned that a lot of service people would be marrying shortly after the war, and it seemed like a good chance it could be our William R Griffiths.

11:31    I replied that William was at No.8 School of Technical Training at RAF Weeton at that time. This was just outside of Blackpool and about 20 miles north of the Liverpool North district, so not too far away.

11:35        A long e-mail from Gregory. He and Paul were making progress on identifying the crash site of the Lancaster, and he considered that it would be fitting to erect a monument there once it had finally been accurately located. With that in mind he thought we should make some efforts to track down the families of the other six crew members. After all it could not possibly take as long to find them as it had done to find William.

11:37        I replied that I would make a start straight away. Taking a break from the never ending roundabout that I was trapped on looking for William's wife might just spark some new idea of how to finally make some progress. I would be leaving S H Lincoln, the second pilot, till last as I did not have good access to records for New Zealand.

11:42        An e-mail from DI, she thought Lincoln's relatives were already known, and she was right. The Auckland Museum in New Zealand had his story in great detail. She was more worried about the Scotsman, McKelvie. Neither of us spotted who would turn out to be the really troublesome one!

15:24        I had a remarkably easy time with the family of Edward Ernest Patchett. Although he had married in the second quarter of 1939 his wife Lily Edna had not had any children. I sent messages to Patchett's niece Sandra and two of her children through Facebook, and contacted a nephew through the Ancestry message system. I told them all the brief outline of Williams' story and his connection to their uncle Edward.

10th December 11:47  I emailed the team with a full family tree for E E Patchet and the news that I had already reached out to his relatives.

18:03  I e-mailed the team, I had received a reply from Patchett's nephew whom I had contacted through Ancestry, it was the right chap and he knew a little about his Uncle Edward's RAF career. I sent him a copy of my brief family tree and more of the details of Edward's RAF story. Less than 31 hours! I also updated them on my efforts to find Oliver Percy Beswick's family. Oliver had married in 1940, but the couple had not had any children. His brother, Edward James, was proving to be both elusive and confusing I the only thing that I could be sure about was that he had died in the Welshpool area in 1989. I found his marriage to Emily Hall in 1934 and ten children born to Beswick-Hall families but none in a place that I could find this couple living.

I did have some reasonably good leads on his sister Elsie. I found her death in 1999 in Bromsgrove and two marriages, the second one in 1963, so unlikely to have produced any children. There was a daughter from her first marriage, and since she had the unusual given name of Averil I was able to easily find her marriage and three children.

13th December 07:30  An e-mail from Di. She had spent some time looking for Alastair Macnab McKelvie, but both of us were less familiar with Scottish records, and the indexes to them gave fewer clues, making it necessary to buy the actual certificate to be sure that the right person was being followed.

10:53  I e-mailed a short update to the team. I had moved on from the Beswick family being in no way close to finding anyone to contact, but I was having even more problems with N R Hartley. I simply could not find his birth record anywhere. I had found him on the 1939 Register Living in the home of a 50 year old widow called Frances Ashton and a John Hartley born in 1919 but listed as a female. There was a pencilled note next to the name which said Jean, so she could have been Norman's wife or sister, and her surname had been amended to Lennon in the same ink as a marginal note "M". I took that to mean that she had married an unknown Mr Lennon sometime after 1939. But I could not find that marriage, nor her birth, nor a marriage between N R Hartley and an unknown Jean.

With his middle name of Rhodes, I was beginning to think that he had been born overseas, probably in the southern parts of Africa.

20:15        Di emailed the team, she was not making any progress tracking down Mr Hartley either.

22:36        I had spent the time since I last updated the team looking for the family of the pilot, Ralph Edward Clark. I expected to have to work my way through quite a few leads to several 'wrong' Clark families as it is not an uncommon name, but at the beginning it was all fairly straightforward.

I found that he had three brothers and two sisters. Neither of the sisters married, and sadly two of his brothers had also died on active service in World War Two. I could find no marriages for any of the three. That just left Alan George Clark born in 1913. I could find no records for him anywhere. I updated the team.

14th December 18:53   John e-mailed the team. Our William Griffiths had not joined the RAF Escaping Society, theirs was a different William Griffiths, so we would not be getting any help from there.

I was to spend the time until the New Year slowly researching the families of the remaining crew members and family matters. Apart from a round of e-mails to and from the team mutually wishing us all a good Christmas and a happy New Year, things became unusually quiet.

That would not last long.

# Chapter 22

## The Second Mystery Photograph

1st January 2019 12:19 Paul e-mailed Gwynn to wish him a happy New Year and included an update on the team's progress. There was little to report with respect to William, but he and Gregory had managed to get a much clearer idea of where the Lancaster came to earth on the 3rd of June. They had found several contacts in the immediate location and would be continuing to interview eye-witnesses (or their families) to try to pin down the exact place.

16:53 Paul forwarded the reply he had received from Gwynn. He had been busy since moving house, and with Christmas too he had simply forgotten to forward the mystery photograph. The picture was on his Smartphone, which he did not, as a rule, use for e-mailing.

He commented that William looked a lot older, and was no longer a sergeant but had been promoted to Warrant Officer. Also he had found a small note book belonging to Ann. There was an entry that said "Will missing June 3rd 1942. Found at Gibraltar July 17th 1942."

16:56 We all finally got to see the mystery picture from Gwynn. That in and of itself makes this a very happy New Year.

William with the 'mystery woman' and child.       Courtesy Gwynn Griffiths

17:37          I e-mailed the team. To me he looked to be around forty years old, which would put it close to the time he left the RAF. I also did not think that the house was in the Penrhyndeudraeth area. It was a terraced house and from the shadow line high up on the wall the picture had been taken either early in the morning or near sunset, and since there were windows open, I thought evening time to be the more likely. So the house was facing East in a terraced row on an almost due North/South alignment with another terrace immediately to the rear. I could find no streets like that in the area.

18:23          Di replied.    The woman's outfit seemed to her to be more like late 1940s or early 1950s. She also commented that men coming out of the war always seemed a lot older than one might normally expect.  She also reminded us that the woman could simply be resident at the house William was billeted or lodging in showing off her new infant. William was not, after all, wearing a wedding ring.

20:56          Paul e-mailed his observations. He knew that William had been promoted to Warrant Officer in July 1958, and was in the Far East between September 1959 and late August 1961, which would be a few months before his discharge from the RAF. It was unlikely that he would continue to wear his uniform after that.

That left a fairly narrow window during which the picture could have been taken. Since the child in it seemed to be between one and two years old that also limited the possible birth dates for the child. Probably the first quarter of 1956 through to the first quarter of 1961, that covers the period from two years before his promotion to one year before he was discharged. This did include the time when he was in East Asia so we were still no nearer discovering where the marriage and the birth of the child may have occurred.

He too was concerned that William was not wearing a wedding ring. He also wondered what the two short vertical stripes on the uniform sleeve signified.

2nd January 00:32    I replied to Paul that I recalled two "Good Conduct" mentions on his service record, but I was not familiar with WW2 RAF uniforms. Certainly they were not similar to good conduct stripes on WW1 army uniform, with which I was more familiar. I would be checking later in the day.

11:51    I managed a more considered e-mail to the team than the one in the early hours of the morning. I had done some research and examined a lot of pictures of RAF uniforms. I concluded that the style that William was wearing in the photograph was superseded on 7th March 1948. The lowest button was dispensed with, as were the two lower pockets, although these pockets were restored a few years later.

That would not really happen overnight as officers had to buy their own uniforms and often had them tailor made. From his service record I could see that he had been promoted to Temporary Warrant Officer in December 1943, but reverted to Aircraftman Second Class on the 8th of March 1948. The picture must have been taken between the end of 1943 and 1948. So he would have been less than 30 years old in the picture. He looked to me to be a lot older than that; he had not worn well at all.

14:16    Paul e-mailed a picture of a RAF

jacket from the period that he had found on-line, the jacket was for sale. It featured a Good Conduct stripe. Just like the WW1 army uniforms that I was more familiar with; these were inverted chevrons applied close to the cuff. The two vertical stripes were not Good Conduct stripes.

18:23          After a very busy time trawling the internet and filtering out much of the dross to be found there, I had found that William's uniform sported two Wound Stripes. But that little snippet only brought up more questions than it answered. Not many RAF personnel seemed to bother with them, and were only given for wounds received on active duty and directly caused by enemy action. We only knew of the one occasion when William was wounded during the night-fighter attack that brought his Lancaster crashing down. On his return to duty in August 1942 he was no longer on front line duties so was very unlikely to have received a second qualifying wound.

Had he claimed for damaging his teeth when landing heavily by parachute? That seemed like a bit of a stretch, and was part of the same engagement that caused to wound to his arm. If he was just out to create a good impression then why was he not wearing his Mentioned in Dispatches Oak Leaf which was his most impressive award?

I had thought that the woman's outfit was late 40s to early 50s, the wide collar was simply too large for the period of clothes rationing during the war. Although this was not completely ended until 1949 some of the restrictions were relaxed after 1945, and bolder fashions quickly started to reappear. My wife, Elaine, also thought that time frame to be the most likely. The lady's hairstyle was also likely to have been from that time.

This was the photograph which we had hoped would help to solve all of our difficulties, just like finding his sister should have done, and later on we were sure that his nephew Gwynn would have been able tell us all we needed to know. His mother Ann's reticence to share any of her early history had precluded that too. It just seemed that every hard won step forward only served to deepen the mystery, and presented us with still more problems to solve.

I e-mailed all of this to the rest of the team and ended with *"One reason that I do this kind of research is that every scrap of information gets to raise more questions than it answers, and the whole picture becomes more and more confused and contradictory until some otherwise insignificant little fact magically solves all the riddles. I don't think we are quite there yet!"*

18:32        Di posted a photograph of an airman that she had previously researched, he looked to be much the same age as William was in the new photograph. But this other fellow had been killed in action aged just 22. It would seem that the picture could have been taken at any time after his return to duty in late 1942 after all.

19:34        Paul e-mailed, he had found an entry on William's service record for a short stay in hospital in Kirkham, which is north of Liverpool, in 1949.

19:44        Di replied that he was at Weeton around that time at No. 10 School of Technical Training. The two places are not far apart, and just a few miles from Blackpool.

19:59        Di had found a possible marriage in the Bootle area, not far from Blackpool, with a likely looking daughter born later on, both had fairly uncommon given names.

20:01        Paul e-mailed that he had already bought that certificate, and unfortunately it was not our William.

4th January 14:09        Paul had been in correspondence with the RAF Changi Association, William had served there in 1958 and 1959 when he was a Warrant Officer. They had no information that could help us. He also asked for some thoughts on his service record. He was unsure whether there was a change from Temporary Warrant Officer in March 1948. The entry simply stated AC2.

14:19        I confirmed that AC2 was a lower rank, Aircraftman Grade 2, and almost as low as you could go, but it probably reflected the large scale reorganisation of the RAF after the war ended.

5th January 16:28        Paul sent two group photographs of members of 205 Squadron taken at RAF Changi that he had received from the Far East Air Forces Association taken some time in the 1950s. William was serving there from 1953 to 1956 and again from 1958.

One had around 120 men in front of a Sunderland flying boat and the other one about 95 servicemen in a more formal pose. The small scale of the photographs and numbers of men made identifying William, even if we were sure he was included in the pictures, practically impossible.

6th January 14:48        Paul forwarded an e-mail he had received from an ex-RAF contact of his. He in turn had been in touch with a fellow 205/209 squadron airman who confirmed from his own collection of records that William was a Master Air Gunner, and later promoted to Warrant Officer at the time when the Sunderland flying boats operating out of Seletar were involved in the bombing of Chin Peng's irregular forces in what was known as the 'Malayan Emergency,' a nasty jungle war against a previous ally that left its mark on everyone involved.

William did another stint in the Far East in 1960 to 1961, this time in the Shackleton Maritime Reconnaissance aircraft based in Tengah.

7th January 18:12        Another e-mail from Paul, his contacts at the RAF Changi Association had not brought us anything new. They only knew of a different William Griffiths. He was hoping that he could find a way to apply for William Richard Griffiths' service records in Gwynn's name. As a close relative the blanked out sections would be revealed to him, and we might then be able to move forward.

          18:24         Di also thought that the full service record would be the only way forward, and there followed a few more e-mails back and forth in the same vein. I will admit that I took little part in that. I knew that it would probably provide the answers that we needed, but it was not always a quick service. Depending on the number of enquiries it could take over a month, and sometimes even longer to receive the service records. I wanted to find something we could all get to work on a bit sooner than that.

8th January 20:11        Paul had been looking through William's family tree and had found out a little more about his uncle Ellis Parry Davies. It looked likely that he had married quite late in life to a Barbara Davies, and there were several possible children for the couple.

23:25          I replied that Ellis was William's uncle, so his children would have been cousins to William, and around 30 years younger than him. I considered that they would have been less likely than Gwynn to have kept in close touch.

9th January 23:48          Paul had turned up some more information, and though it was useful, it was certainly not pleasant reading. In November 1966 there was a newspaper report from Chester Magistrates Court, a William Richard Griffiths of Hoole Road in Chester had pleaded guilty to trying to steal some small items from a local Chemist's shop. The age given matched our man. He was given a conditional discharge as he had no previous convictions and had been receiving treatment at the Deva Hospital for alcoholism and nerves.

A second report in the Observer newspaper from 21st April 1967 said that a William Richard Griffiths of no fixed address had stolen a watch from the Chester Probation Office. He stated that he had been 'under duress' and had been receiving treatment at Moston and Denbigh Hospitals. This time our man would be going to prison for three months.

Paul added that there remained just a slight possibility that these reports were for a different William Richard Griffiths. Although there were no William Richard Griffiths born in the area at the right time, there was a record for a Richard William Griffiths born in Edge Hill Lancashire who died in Halton near Chester in 1995. Overall though the progression did seem to be both logical and typical, alcoholism, hospital, prison then sheltered accommodation.

It all seemed to fit too well with what we had discovered back in July the previous year. I was then, and still am, of the opinion that William was a man stretched beyond his limits.

He had gone to war in and entirely unsuitable and dangerously unreliable aircraft. His position in the lonely, bitterly cold, cramped confines of the rear gun turret was the most dangerous on the aircraft. Any attacking night fighter would always aim to approach from behind and try to eliminate the possibility of return fire from the rear gunner as soon as possible.

There had been at least eight aircraft and their crews lost during his time on 61 Squadron, not counting his own. He would have known most, if not all, of those airmen. I was sure that he carried a heavy burden of responsibility for the loss of those six men of his own crew, especially Norman Hartley. I felt that he had simply seen one too many deaths. It should not come as a surprise that a normal, middle class, quiet life would never be his.

10th January 01:15     Following on from finding that William was in the area at the time Paul had found a marriage between a William R Griffiths and a Miss Griffith in Birkenhead in the early 70s. There were several children that might have been their offspring.

11:46           I replied that the newspaper reports that Paul had found were almost certainly our William Richard Griffiths. We knew that he had ended up in a hostel for homeless men in Fazackerly. I thought that he may have been somewhat institutionalised by his long service in the RAF, and struggling with alcohol problems, which may have had something to do with some long term poor health issues or injuries since he was discharged in 1962 as being medically unfit.

I said that if Paul had good feeling that the marriage in Birkenhead could be our William R Griffiths, he should apply for the certificate. I did not think that that it was a particularly promising one for several reasons. 1971 would have been too late for the family photograph and there were two local William R Griffiths, one born in 1928 and the other in 1941 who would have been much more likely.

I did pass on the address and phone number of the relevant Register Office and say that they should be able to provide the answer before he parted with his cash.

14:06        A further e-mail from Paul, the Richard William Griffiths that died in Halton in 1995 had left a will. He thought it unlikely that the unfortunate Griffiths in the late 60s newspaper reports would have anything to bequeath. So our William Richard Griffiths was probably the one in those reports.

14:50        Di replied that she too agreed, and commented that, for the time being at least, this was not the sort of information that we should be passing on to nephew Gwynn.

16:52        Paul had contacted the Chester Family History Society, he would be asking if they had access to the local Electoral Rolls for the time that William was thought to be in the area. Coincidentally they used to hold their meetings in Hoole Road. He had also been checking maps and images of the area to see if he could find somewhere resembling our mystery photograph.

18:22        I replied that I too had been checking for likely looking houses. I had looked at some candidates in the area. The streets ran in the right direction and the distance between the backs of the houses seemed about right. But if the window styles matched, then the rear wall was the wrong height, or the extension had a different type of pitched roof. I could find no close match at all.

11th January 12:47     Paul had received a reply from the archivist of 205 Squadron. The fairly basic, not to say primitive, conditions in Changi with the high temperatures and high humidity may well have led a chap in his 40s serving there to develop too much of a taste for the local beer, especially if he was there on his own. A long service in the RAF 'family' coming to such an abrupt end could also have been part of the reason William found himself in such poor circumstances.

He had also heard back from the Cheshire Archives. They would be checking the court records and Electoral Rolls. They mentioned that there had been a sheltered home or hostel on Hoole Road at the time.

14:04          I had found a reference, in Hansard of all places, to the Helping Hand Organisation and their Hostel at 27 Hoole Road Chester, it had room for 12 people.

I also said that I had worked with a few chaps who did part of their National Service in Changi and Tengah, in the early 60s. They were much less polite about the conditions there, but I don't think that their comments should appear in print.

I decided that it might be worthwhile trying to find some more information from Helping Hand, but they appeared to have gone out of existence. I did find a charity with the same name operating in a different location, but it was recently established and there was no connection. I found two more charities with very similar names, but again no connection, and although they were helping the local disadvantaged, neither had ever run any residential centres.

The fourth lead seemed very promising, a very similar name and in the right area, but it was in fact not a charity but a chain of private nursing and old people's homes, so we were still no further forward.

14:24   Paul had passed the Charity's details on to his Cheshire local history connections and was hoping they might have been able to could come up with some records.

15:15   I forwarded on to the team what I had found concerning the Helping Hand Organisation.

15:32   Paul was wondering if it would be useful, or even possible to get the relevant prison records and if they might provide any clues to his family, or even confirm for certain that we were still following the right William Richard Griffiths.

17:05   I responded to Paul's earlier e-mail that we would not be able to access the prison records for this period. I had found a small selection on-line but nothing after 1971.

We had now reached a very low point in the search for our man's wife and children. There was the tantalizing clue of the photograph, which alongside the questions that it had inevitably raised had failed to provide any answers as we might have reasonably expected it to. This picture of itself did not of course prove that there had actually been a marriage, but other explanations seemed to have been a little unlikely. Yet we remained unable to make any really meaningful progress. We were all, at this point, at a loss for any clear path forward and each of us grasping for different straws.

I remained convinced that while the picture held the key, the catalyst that would enable us to unlock the puzzle had been overlooked, misinterpreted or was yet to be discovered. Even though I had already been over much of this ground before I would be doing so again. I just wish I could master the trick of seeing it all with completely fresh eyes.

Paul was pursuing the connections that William had to Cheshire and Liverpool. Quite early in the search we found out that he had an uncle who was married near there in 1905, and although the family had subsequently moved to America, there may have been more relatives there that we had not discovered. We knew for certain that William had died in Liverpool, and it looked highly probable that he had lived in Chester soon after his discharge from the RAF. It was not unlikely that a man somewhat down on his luck would be trying to reconnect with members of his extended family.

I thought it likely that Di and John were also quietly following their own paths and trying to find any possible way forward.

14th January 13:41    Paul had had a reply from the Cheshire County Archive. They had found William in private lodgings at 11 Hoole Road on the 1967 Electoral Rolls for just the one year. They would need more time to access the court records from their offsite storage, but they would be very unlikely to tell us anything that we did not already know. They also had the old records from Deva Hospital, which had now changed its name to the Countess of Chester Hospital, but they had nothing later than 1959.

15th January 14:33     With so few other leads to follow, Paul had applied for the William R Griffiths marriage certificate in Birkenhead in 1971 even though we all thought it to be very unlikely that it was our William. Without doubt the mounting sense of desperation that we were all feeling had a role to play in that decision. Now the certificate had arrived. It was indeed not our William.

16th January 11:40     Paul forwarded a reply that he had just received from the RAF Museum. They had identified the Warrant Officer Class 1 badge on the left sleeve as the style which was superseded in 1946. They also confirmed the two vertical stripes as being wound stripes. To me this put us firmly back to the 1943-1946 period where we had looked so hard for a marriage close to the Caernarfon and Pwllheli area at the end of the previous November. I could not see what we had missed then.

17th January 17:35     Paul had found a family tree on Ancestry that had William's grandfather John and many of his living descendants. He sent a link to that tree, and said that he would be contacting the tree owner to see if he had any more information than we did. There were some slight differences and Paul was asking why I had the birth date for this John Griffiths as 1852 when from the census records shown on my tree he should have been born in 1853 or 1854.

I started to check through both of these trees, my own one of our William and this new one on Ancestry, with slightly mixed feelings. I thought that it was an unnecessary distraction and would just waste time. On the other hand it gave me something new to get my teeth into, and I would enjoy this small challenge.

17:45          Paul e-mailed a link to a photograph

on this new tree of a Gomer Griffiths, he would have been a cousin to William. There was a distinct likeness to our man. Furthermore this chap died in Liverpool, reinforcing the possibility of strong links to the area.

19:13        Di replied that when we had found the earlier connection of an uncle of William's in Toxteth the local records office had confirmed that there were many Welsh families in the area at the time. She did not see that we would be discovering any relatives closer than nephew Gwynn from this new tree.

18th January 18:02      I e-mailed the team with the results of my checks so far. Paul was correct about the birth date, from the 1861 census that we had for our John Griffiths he could have been born between April 8th 1853 and April 7th 1854. But calculating ages from the census dates is not that straightforward. The column should show the age in complete years for the person at the time of the census.

Any slight lack of skill in numeracy on the part of the person filling in the form could easily put the age one year out. If there was any misunderstanding of the 'complete year' rule this could have the same result. For a native Welsh speaker who may not be highly literate this could also be a problem as the instructions were in English only. This was probably the case as on the later censuses his age sometimes differed by a year. Hence I considered that the possible birth dates for our John ranged from 1852 to 1855.

There were five possible births in the area, and I included a list of those, but none in 1852 so that would always serve to remind me that I had not fixed his birth date. As I had not planned to go any further back to his parents and siblings, I did not see that should cause any problems. I would be continuing to check to make sure that we had the right John Griffiths.

18:42         Paul had had a reply from the new tree owner. He believed that we had the same John Griffiths in the two trees. He had not heard mention of William Richard Griffiths, but his own father had connections to both Liverpool and Birkenhead. More indications that our William may have gone to Cheshire, and later Liverpool, because of extended family connections there.

19th January 11:58        I updated the team on my researches. Morris Griffiths' father John was on the 1881 census with his wife Ann and their eldest son Griffith living in Llanenddwyn, and gave his place of birth as Llanddwywe. The family were still altogether on the 1891 census, and then on the 1901 census when all six children, Griffith, John, Robert, Richard, William and Morris, were all still living in Lanenddwyn. John was a joiner on all of these censuses.

The John Griffiths from the new tree is also on the 1881 Census. He was living in Llanddwywe with his wife Mary and their children William and Robert. John was a Blacksmith and their address was given as The Smithy in Talybont. He was also a blacksmith on the 1871 census when he was living with his father William who was a Master Smith and his elder brother John, who was also a Blacksmith. The family was living in Llanddwywe.

I could certainly see that the two Johns may easily be confused, both are born within a year or so in the tiny hamlet of Llanddwywe which is only a mile from the equally tiny hamlet of Llanenddwyn, and to the non-Welsh speaker the two could look like the same place. Our John, a Joiner, was on the 1901 census with a Morris Griffiths who was the right

140

age to be our William Richard Griffith's father. The other John, the Blacksmith, does not appear on any census with a child called Morris.

20th January 18:50    Paul replied. He agreed that they were certainly two different John Griffiths in spite of the new tree owner's assertions to the contrary. They might well be distantly related given the small population and the size of the villages. Which led him on to raise the questions that we had all been trying to answer.

Was the William Richard Griffiths in the newspaper reports our William? He was still inclined to think so. Did he ever marry? His view was that he did not marry after his discharge in 1962. Could we be sure that he was the William Griffiths who died in Fazackerly Hospital? He would have been more comfortable with that if we had been able to find a better connection to the area.

21st January 00:27    I replied to Paul's e-mail that the odds of all the Griffiths in the area being related was not quite as straight forward as one might imagine.

The way the old Welsh Patronymic naming system worked some of the Griffiths would have descended from families whose family name was Griffiths, as you would expect in England, but not all of these would be closely related. Others would have descended from a Griffith Whatever, the Griffiths standing for 'child of Griffith' so completely random family names and not necessarily a close connection. This patronymic naming still has effects on Welsh genealogy and can be a real pain.

I said that I thought he should continue to talk to this new tree owner though, as negative information is sometimes just as valuable as positive.

I also said that I was 85% convinced that the newspaper reports were for our William, I would need some persuading that it was not him. I was more sure about the Death Certificate. The birth date made it very likely; and his RAF number gave rock solid confirmation.

I agreed that it was most unlikely that he had married after 1962. He may have married before 1947, and the mother and child photo would seem to be fairly good confirmation of that, though that does not indicate that the marriage lasted. Right from the start when we found that he was living in the Field Lane Centre we knew that his life post RAF had been sad, possibly isolated and definitely chaotic. He should have had the means to live a more comfortable life.

There are many things that could have had a bearing on this. He may have been sufficiently institutionalized by 20 years service to be not entirely comfortable running his own affairs. Alcohol was almost certainly a factor. But more than anything he reminded me of one of my close in-law's uncle George.

He struggled to cope with civilian life when he left the forces; he was in the RAF and later NATO working on Westland Whirlwinds. Eventually he moved in with his sister. Because he then had family to live with his life was not so chaotic, but he was still very 'semi-detached', partly because he was institutionalized and had a drink problem, but mostly because he was what was politely called at the time 'a confirmed bachelor'.

We may not have been able to find William's marriage because there was no marriage. He may even have arranged the photo of the daughter of the house where he was lodging with her baby to show big sister Ann that he had found good family digs.

I ended with *'Whatever the truth of it all, and no one will ever know the full story, just because he was a hero does not give us the right to think that he must be a perfect model of the 'English Gentleman', he was who he was and played his part as well as he was able. I still salute him.'*

# Chapter 23

## Our Quarry is Sighted

21st January 01:53    A short, but very telling, e-mail from John. He pointed out that William's RAF service number had not been quoted anywhere in relation to his death.

11:40        I replied that John was absolutely right. When I had serious difficulties with a project in the past it usually proved to be because either some small nugget that I've attached no importance to or more often an erroneous assumption that I had made. At last I knew what I should be looking for.

12:14        An update to the team. When William had applied for his Caterpillar Club membership in 1944 he was at Penrhos near Pwlleli, his service record shows him there from late November 1943 through to July 1944 with No 9 Advanced Flying Unit, probably teaching air gunnery in the Ansons stationed at Llandwrog. He was a temporary Warrant Officer at the time, and the prime period for a marriage to the mystery woman.

I had ruled out all of the North Wales marriages that I had found previously. I would be repeating those searches. I would be trying to establish which marriages we might have ruled out incorrectly, and which ones were worth more serious consideration.

I also noticed that on his service record when the Children's Names and Dates of Birth block has been covered over (as we would have expected) there was a faint pencil tick mark to show that the information in that box had been checked. I wondered if that indicated that there actually was some information in that box to be checked, or that the fact that there was no information had been confirmed as correct. I now believed the former to be most likely, so there was indeed a wife and children to be discovered.

This was exactly the same thing that I had advised Paul to look out for on the service record back in December!

12:26        Paul had been checking the marriages in the area for that period too. He had found a highly probable candidate. It was Katie Hughes yet again! He had applied for the certificate direct from the Register Office.

12:28        Di replied that she was away from her records and could not confirm for certain but thought that this marriage had already been checked out and was not our William.

12:34        I added that I had bought that certificate, and I had specified that the Groom's middle name must be Richard and his father's name must be Morris, they had sent the certificate in spite of the fact that neither of these conditions was met. I was able to get my cash back after a few weeks of complaining. This was definitely not our William.

15:02        I e-mailed everyone. I now had three possible marriages. Two in the last quarter of 1943, one to an Ellen Roberts and the other to a Katie Williams these two seemed the most promising as they were close to where William was stationed at the time. I thought that I might have already ruled these two out by speaking to the Registrar for the district, but not could find any notes about that, so I had to assume for the time being that I did not.

When I saw the last one I had to do a double take. I had misread it as Barbara Beswick, Had he married his crew mate's widow, sister or some other relative? What a coincidence that would be. The name however was Bestwick and should prove to be an easy name to research. The marriage had taken place in early 1944 in the St Asaph registration district, quite a bit further away from his base.

I would be asking my friendly registrar about the 1943 marriages in the morning, as they were both within her district. The St Asaph one would take a bit more work, the Registration district had been closed and the registers split between three districts. But there were two possible children for this marriage that had been registered in St Asaph and another two later on in the Wirral district, which is just a little further to the east.

22nd January 10:15    I telephoned my helpful Registrar in North Wales, but she was away for a few days. I sent a detailed e-mail instead. Typically just when we have a hot new trail to follow and are desperate to start making progress again something crops up to slow us down.

15:54    Paul had an e-mail from the General Register Office. They wanted to know if he still required the certificate that he had ordered even though it was not William Richard Griffiths. He had, of course, declined.

23rd January 20:08    Paul had also been checking through William's RAF service record. He had found out that William had been discharged at the end of May 1946 to the reserves, and in March 1948 he had re-enlisted as a regular in the RAF.

23:07    I replied that would certainly be a much more likely explanation for William's demotion from

Temporary Warrant Office to Aircraftman Class 2.

I also updated the team on my progress with the possible marriage and children. It was starting to look like William had married Barbara Bestwick in the first quarter of 1944 in the St Asaph district. There were two children on the birth indexes for a Griffiths - Bestwick couple also in St Asaph, the first was a Susan M registered in the last quarter of 1944 and a David P L registered in the last quarter of 1946.

Sadly there was also a Susan M Griffiths aged three listed on the death index for 1947. If that was indeed William and Barbara's daughter the effect on them both must have been very severe.

Then I found a record of a Barbara Griffiths and her son David as passengers on the Empire Trooper going to Singapore in early 1954, both ages given for the pair tallied with their birth dates, ominously there was no Susan with them. This was shortly after William's posting there and I would normally have thought that neatly tied up the whole story. In this case however there was also a Sylvia Griffiths aged one travelling with Barbara and David.

On checking the birth indexes a likely looking Sylvia had been born in Wrexham in 1952, but her mother's maiden name was given as Lloyd. I was still waiting for a reply from the local Register Office, but in the mean time I would be checking for a different Barbara Griffiths with children David and Sylvia.

As it turned out I did not do any such research. Shortly after I sent that last e-mail I began to have trouble accessing anything on the Internet. Since it was by then after midnight, I decided to call it a day and pick up where I left off the following morning.

24th January 10:15     I was still having serious problems trying to get anything to work on-line. After hours of trying I had figured out that the only websites I could access were the BBC, although none of the images would display, the on-line vets I used to get the dog's medicines and Facebook. I could neither send nor receive e-mail.

I had tried several trace-routes and any request I sent out always seemed to arrive at the correct destination but no reply was ever issued. Classically it had taken me until just minutes after the close of office hours to discover all of this and my Internet Service Provider's 9 to 5 support line had all gone home. Many rude words were uttered.

17:35     I realised that I still had a small lifeline. At the end of October the previous year I had exchanged messages on Facebook with Di, it was done as just a bit of fun showing off that I could find people if given a few clues. I sent her a message, my internet connection was broken and I could not research or use e-mail. I asked her to update the rest of the team and whether I needed to respond to any messages.

Since the only research option left open to me was Facebook I spent a lot of time trying to find pages for the people that we had recently indentified. There were enough possibilities to keep me busy for quite a while. But I was not able to confidently identify anyone we were looking for there.

17:37     Di sent a copy of an e-mail from John. He did not regard the Lloyd maiden name as an absolute reason to rule out Sylvia, such mistakes were all too common.

17:48          I replied that I had also seen that on quite a few occasions. I added that I would have to telephone my friendly Registrar in the morning since she would be trying to e-mail me about the marriages and births.

17:50          Di had found a possible marriage for David Griffiths in the Bristol area, and also a possible son.

18:01          I messaged Di. I had seen a marriage for a Barbara Griffiths when I was searching for Electoral Roll entries just before my internet connection died. I had not thought it to be particularly interesting at that time as it was in Bristol, but if there was a connection to the area, it might be worth following up. I thought that it would have been in the 1960s or 70s from memory.

I added that although the marriage to Barbara Bestwick looked highly likely, especially in the light of the trip she took to Singapore, William would have been stationed over an hour's drive away from the St Asaph district at the time.

This was never an easy trip with narrow roads and some serious bottlenecks on the way, a bit of a long haul for every day. However, as he was at a training unit he may have been at home at weekends and stayed at the mess during the week.

20:24          Paul e-mailed the team (I would receive this on the evening of the 25th) He had found a marriage for Sylvia Griffiths and her new husband's family name should be an easy one to research. Could I look for her on Facebook? He was also asking the team's opinion as to what we tell Gwynn, and when, about his newly found cousin.

I then checked Facebook looking for Sylvia under her married name, there were just three possibilities. Two of these had their Friends list visible, but I could not find any one there whose name fitted with our new list of Sylvia's probable relatives.

The third one had made her friends list private, but her timeline was visible. No-one that I was looking for had posted or reacted to her posts there. All three looked highly unlikely to be our Sylvia.

20:35        Di e-mailed the team. She told them I was having a few problems with e-mail so I might not answer straight away.

# Chapter 24

## And Driven From Cover

25th January 10:25    I had telephoned my friendly Registrar and just as I had half remembered, the two marriages for her area had been ruled out back in November the previous year. The more promising one in St Asaph was outside of her district    so she was not able to look that one up, but she did give me the number of the office in Rhyl where the registers were now kept.

I telephoned them straight away. I told the Registrar a little of William's story and why we had all been looking for him for so long and asked her if the marriage to Barbara Bestwick was indeed our man. Sticking strictly to the disclosure rules, she said that she could not tell me that, but did confirm that she had a marriage certificate for a William Richard Griffiths of the right age whose father was a Morris Griffiths. Would I like to buy that?

We soon sorted the transaction out and I was now the theoretical owner of the marriage certificate that we had all waited so long to see. I was informed that processing the request and producing the copy certificate normally took three or four days and the certificate would then be sent to me by second class post.

I explained why we were so desperate for the information and asked if, since I had now paid for a copy, she could read the details out to me. That too was against the disclosure rules. We would have to wait a few more days yet.

14:54        I was finally back on-line and e-mailed the rest of the team, I quote: *"A FEW PROBLEMS, don't believe another word this woman says. I've spent since midnight Tuesday night with NO email NO web access apart from Facebook, the on-line Vets that I get the dogs medicines from and the BBC (but no images) and a burning desire to track down this Bestwick woman. I have no hair left, nor any fingernails! Apparently someone did a nationwide update of something overnight on Tuesday and whatever anyone sent here it 'lost' my IP address, just mine, not one of the other 66 million people in the country, just mine. Since they can't find out why, they have done a software rollback and I am now online again.*

*Barbara Bestwick had married William Richard Griffiths, son of Morris Griffiths Q1 1944 St Asaph and the certificate is on its way here as I write this, unless it gets lost in the post, spontaneously combusts or is seized and held hostage by the Welsh Liberation Front. Nothing would surprise me now."*

I also listed the three probable children.

15:18        Paul e-mailed; he repeated his mail from the previous evening with the information concerning Sylvia's marriage. Just to rub salt into the wound both of those e-mails arrived together.

15:29        I replied to Paul's e-mail that I would be searching for Sylvia's children but concentrating more on Barbara's family. I also said that it should be fine to tell Gwynn that we thought that we now knew who the woman and child were in his photograph, and that we were on the track of further children.

16:11        I had found an Electoral Roll entry for Sylvia and her husband giving a very recent address, I updated the team.

16:25 Another e-mail from Paul. I am not sure whether his request for a phone number for Sylvia was meant to imply that I was making good progress at last, or lagging behind. I decided that I should take it as the former.

# Chapter 25

## The Hunt Concludes

26th January 11:15     I e-mailed the team. The marriage certificate that I had ordered just over 24 hours previously had turned up in the post. My new favourite Registrar may not have been willing to break the rules, but she certainly knew when to bend them a little. Excellent service. I included a scan of the certificate.

11:59          John e-mailed a link to a local family history website, there were two photographs of Barbara. In one she was with her two older siblings, her brother Bernard in his Army uniform and sister Jean Mary, both girls were in WAAF uniform. He had also found that her brother Bernard had died in Normandy just after D-Day. There was also a younger brother Raymond to add to their family tree.

12:09          I found a comment on the website, the late David Griffiths (William and Barbara's son) had been in the RAF and was the leader of the Falcons Parachute Display Team in 1984.

12:33          I informed the team that I had made a good start on building Barbara's family tree with her parents and siblings, and would be moving on to try to find some contact details for any of them. I would be including Sylvia, but I still harboured reservations about her. The incorrect mother's maiden name on her birth register index was still to be resolved.

12:59          I sent a message to the local history website that John had found. I explained that the Barbara

154

Bestwick who appeared on their site had married our William Richard Griffiths and why we were trying to contact any of their living descendants. I included a link to the BBC news article that outlined Gregory's original request for help.

I asked if it would be possible to pass my contact details on to the chap who had posted the pictures of the Bestwick family. Peter's surname was fairly distinctive, and I soon found out where he fitted into the Bestwick family, he was Jean Mary's son and so a nephew to Barbara. I also had little trouble in finding him on Facebook, and although I checked, I could not find a link there to Sylvia.

13:17        I received an e-mail from Paul, he wanted to know if I would be updating the Griffiths family tree on ancestry.

13:22        I replied that I was actually thinking about uploading a new tree there when his message arrived. I found manually updating an existing tree to be more time consuming than uploading the tree I had on my own PC.

Then I changed my mind. I would be manually updating the on-line tree after all, but would not include any evidence or references to save time. But I was going to continue to try to find contact methods for Sylvia's relatives. Partly to confirm that we were on the right track but also to see if we could get the elusive telephone number for her, we already had a recent address and I had found a few possible folk with Facebook pages.

13:48        I had updated the family tree on Ancestry and had also found a current address and telephone number for Barbara's younger brother Raymond, which I shared with the team. I asked if someone else would like to make the call.

I don't have a high success rate with cold calls, most folk seem to think that I am trying to soften them up for a sales pitch for overpriced useless goods or services, or trying to get their bank account details to fund my lavish lifestyle. This close to a possible successful conclusion to the project I did not want to bring the whole lot crashing down about everyone's ears.

13:52        Paul said he was willing to make the telephone call if no-one else wanted to, though he said it was going to take a while for him to assimilate all the new facts and work out what his approach should be.

14:15        Paul asked if we had found a marriage for William's son David as he could not see her on the updated tree

14:32        I confirmed that Di had found a wife sometime ago, but I had her marked on the tree as 'living' so she was not visible, I changed his permissions to be able to view living persons. We were also researching some possible children for them.

14:37        Paul asked if we had any more background information about Raymond before he made his telephone call. I replied and gave him Raymond's wife's name and their approximate ages and also said I had not found any likely children for them, though I had not searched particularly thoroughly.

By this time I had found the death register index for David, and identified his probable children. I had also found Sylvia's children and knew all of their names, including those of the married daughters. I went back to looking for them on

Facebook, surely one or more of them would lead me to Sylvia.

15:32          Paul sent an e-mail. He had spoken to Marjorie (Raymond's wife). She confirmed that David had died fairly recently and also his wife's name. Marjorie confirmed that they had had children. She had her address, but not immediately to hand and she did not have a telephone number for her.

She went on to talk about Sylvia and verified that we had found the correct marriage for her, and that they had three children. (We had found three too, so they were almost certainly the right ones.) She then gave Paul her address, which was actually the one that we already had, and the telephone number which was what we had been so eager to find out.

She also said that Barbara, David and Sylvia had gone to Singapore when William was first posted there, but not when he went for the second time. She knew that he had a drink problem, and that was part of the reason that the marriage ended. Barbara had later remarried. Marjorie and Raymond often talked about 'Will' and they knew a little of his escape from occupied Europe, but very few of the details.

15:38          I e-mailed Paul, He had done well. I would be adding David's children to the family tree and checking for the new marriages. Using the children's names and a few clues that Marjorie had given I was finally able to find Sylvia's Facebook page. It was not among the three that I had checked out earlier.

17:00          Paul e-mailed with just a brief note. He had spoken to Sylvia and everything was fine, but she was waiting to receive an e-mail from him outlining what we had found. After he had sent that he would be fully updating us all. I immediately replied with congratulations and to add that I had now found most of the family on Facebook.

18:04          A very long e-mail arrived from Paul. He forwarded a copy of the message that he sent to Sylvia to us all and added some extensive notes about their telephone conversation. She had last seen her father in the early 1960s so probably just after he left the RAF. She had hidden from him as he was fairly drunk and disruptive, which was not unusual.

After her mother's death she had tried to find out more about her father, but had made no progress and had eventually given up. She was sure that the newspaper articles concerning William's court appearances were indeed referring to her father.

She had no idea where and when he had died and naturally was very upset to learn that had been in such sad circumstances. She knew about her sister Susan Mary's tragic death at just under three years old. She was delighted when Paul told her that she had a cousin Gwynn. She also said that she had William's RAF escape 'purse' and his Caterpillar Club badge. She would be taking some time to digest all the new information that we had so suddenly given to her.

In his e-mail to Sylvia, Paul had included the family tree we had built up and drew attention to William's sister Ann and her son Gwynn, Sylvia's new cousin.

He also provided links to the article in the Cambrian Times and explained that the Belgian gentleman "Greg" mentioned in the newspaper articles had been the driving force behind our researches.

He had concluded with *"On behalf of the research team (five of us in total) I would like to say again thank you so much for speaking to me. We passionately believe the actions of men like your father shouldn't be forgotten and that is why undertook this research - to remember him."*

# Chapter 26

## Reflections

Right from the start of this search I had known that I was looking for a tail-gunner of a shot down Lancaster bomber who had managed to escape from occupied Europe back to Britain. That qualified him as a hero in my book. I also knew, from the sad circumstances of his death, that he probably had a serious problem with alcohol addiction and had drifted into the margins of society. I suspected that he would have been a difficult man to know.

Did any of that make him less of a hero to me? Not at all. From my comfortable, safe situation I would never be in a position to make such a harsh judgement. I always thought that I was looking at a man who had simply seen one too many deaths. The death of his father when William was still so young must have affected him deeply. Furthermore his life with his new step-father may not have been as happy and trouble free as anyone might have hoped. His only sister Ann went away to live with her Aunt Gwen. That's a lot for a child to deal with.

During his RAF service he had many more deaths to deal with. We know he was at 25 OTU when several fatalities occurred. While he was on 61 Squadron eight complete crews were lost. 56 men he had known, including his own co-pilot's brother. Yet still he and his crew continued to fly their assigned missions.

The rear turret of any bomber was a cold and lonely place to be in the dark above enemy held territory. At an altitude of 15,000 feet the temperature could well be down to below minus 30°C even in the summer time. To help to deal with that he had several layers of heavy, bulky clothing, although these would make his job harder if he needed to clear a jammed gun. He also had the option of an electrically heated suit and gloves. Not many gunners chose to use the hot suit.

After six or more hours staring intently into the dark night both dreading and hoping to see the faintest glimmer of an approaching enemy aircraft, it was all too easy to drift off into reverie, or even fall asleep. Keeping uncomfortably cold was just one of the ways that aircrew used to combat that.

Some went even further. The Perspex turret glazing could often make the gunner's job harder. It was prone to distracting and misleading reflections and refractions, and would ice over when the conditions were unfavourable. To help alleviate these problems they fitted 'clear vision panels'. Well, actually they simply removed one or more sections of the glazing, and lost what little barrier there was between themselves and the arctic cold at high altitude.

Tail-gunners were the most vulnerable of all the crew. Almost all attacks by enemy fighters would be carried out from behind, and usually below, the bomber. The attacking pilot would bring his nose up sharply to fire into the rear turret while immediately pushing the nose of his aircraft down slightly so the hits moved forward towards the centre of the bomber, then along one wing to knock out the engines and set fire to the fuel tanks located there.

Many rear gunners were dead before any of the crew had time to realise that they were under attack, and even if he survived that first attack, he still had to get out of his turret, find and fit his parachute and safely exit the aeroplane. Any of those tasks could have been made impossible by damage inflicted on the bomber. The fact that William survived this encounter would not mean that he did not find it anything less than extremely traumatic.

I cannot escape the feeling that Sergeant Griffiths probably felt an enormous sense of personal guilt when his Lancaster was shot down. This is not an uncommon feeling for any survivor where other people do not fare so well. Worse still it probably was, in his own mind, his fault.

His job as the Rear Gunner was to protect his aircraft and the crew. He had failed to do that. The fact that he never really stood much chance of success would not have occurred to him, or been thought relevant. He was, as we have seen earlier, out gunned, and although his training had stressed that as his job, the crew's only real chance would come from him warning the pilot of any imminent attack. Bomber pilots were trained to perform a corkscrew manoeuvre when under attack from a fighter aircraft. This involved a violent turn down and to one side, immediately followed by a violent turn back up, usually in the opposite direction.

The German fighter pilots were, of course, well aware of this tactic, and would be ready to follow the bomber. Everything depended on the rear gunner's call to corkscrew, and most importantly in which direction to turn first. Only if this call came at exactly the right time, the ensuing aerial ballet could expose the attacking fighter to fire from the bomber's guns, while being unable to bring his own more powerful weapons to bear. The odds would still be heavily against the bomber, but a lucky burst, at sufficiently close range, into one of the more vulnerable parts just might put an end to the attack. A slim chance, but it was all that they were ever going to have. Our crew did not get even that desperate chance.

Add to all that the fact that after he had been obliged to shove his crew mate Hartley out of the rear door he did not see his parachute open, nor was anything ever discovered about his fate, then those six deaths must have been an immense burden for William to bear.

His return to civilian life in 1946 should have given our man the opportunity to recover some sense of a peaceful normality and slowly heal the wounds of war. He had a new wife, a daughter, another child on the way and a new job. The hope of whole new, brighter, quieter, better future to look forward to. A chance to start afresh. Everything to live for.

But life would not turn out to be that kind to our William. Suddenly on the 4th of August 1947 everything changed. His daughter Susan Mary, not yet three years old, died in a tragic accident.

At the time the family was living in a flat above an amusement arcade in Rhyl owned by William's father-in-law. William had a job in a local shop and Barbara was looking after both Susan and their new baby son. As Susan walked along a passageway in the flat she came to a connecting door to the workshop of the arcade which had been left open. She saw a nice bright, shiny coin in the back of a slot machine undergoing repair. As she reached inside to pick up her new treasure she was fatally electrocuted.

Just one more death to add to William's heavy burden. One so very close to home.

With his resources drained by his experiences in the war this final bitter blow proved to be too much. Now William was set on a roller coaster descent into a self destructive pattern of anger, despair, hopelessness and alcoholism that ultimately brought him to his sad and lonely end. A pattern today we might recognise as Post Traumatic Stress Disorder. Brought on, not as I had previously thought by the deaths of so many of his RAF chums for some of whom he felt personally responsible, though those had undoubtedly pushed him so very close to the brink, but by the entirely accidental death of a child. His own child.

Just one death too many.

He deserved better.

He deserved, at the very least, to be remembered as a brave man who already given too much for his country and his family. A man from whom the war, bad luck and alcohol had taken more than he could cope with and left him an angry, confused and lonely soul. So I still salute him, and I hope I have done a little to give some context to the desperately unhappy years of his later life. That was not the real man underneath all the pain, anger and despair. But it was all the world could see.

All too often our service men and women and their families have to sacrifice more than they should ever be asked for. And that makes him just a forgotten hero who was pushed just a little bit too far and ended up paying a very high price. One among so many unnamed thousands about whom we know so little, but to whom we owe so much. One more casualty of war.

Rest in Peace William, you did your bit as well as anyone could possibly expect.

# Appendix I

## The Clark Crew

**Pilot Officer Ralph Edward Clark** 102988, Pilot

Born in early 1919 in Southampton the son of Walter Thomas Clark and Edith Emily (née Headley) and aged just 23 when he was killed. He had not married. He had three brothers and two sisters. Neither of the sisters married and one of his brothers died as an infant.

His eldest brother was Henry Thomas Clark born in 1904. He never married. He served as a private in the Hampshire regiment and died in Normandy on D-Day.

Philip Charles Headly Clark was born on the 27th of March 1916 in Southampton. He never married. He served in 153 Squadron RAF and was killed on the 1st of March 1945 when Lancaster NG184 crashed into the sea returning from a raid on Mannheim. His body was not recovered.

With no close relatives to track down a first cousin who has lived in Canada for the last 50 years has been traced and informed of his relative's RAF career.

Clark took part in nine operations with 61 Squadron to add to the eight on his time on 144 Squadron where he was awarded the Distinguished Flying Medal.

**Sergeant Stanley Holmes Lincoln** 41342 RNZAF, 2nd pilot

He was the son of Frank and Eileen Agnes Lincoln (née Cronin) from Mount Alberta, Auckland, New Zealand and was born in 1917. He is remembered online on the Auckland War Memorial website.

He enlisted on the same day as his brother, Lloyd John Holmes Lincoln and they had consecutive service numbers. Both served in 61 Squadron. Lloyd was the second pilot in Manchester L7470 flown by Flight Sergeant Noble when it was shot down by Oberleutnant Eckart-Wilhelm von Bonin in a Bf110 night-fighter while they were on the way to raid on Essen on the night of 6/7th of April 1942. This was his third operational trip, the entire seven man crew died.

It must have taken a great deal of both courage and resolve for Stanley to continue his active service after the loss of his brother; he was in action over Hamburg just two nights later. Stanley had taken part in 10 operational sorties.

A relative has been traced and informed of our findings.


**Sergeant Edward Ernest Patchett** 1053543, navigator

Born on the 5th of January 1914 in Frizinghall, Yorkshire the son of Ernest and his wife Ada (neé Murby). Edward married Lily Edna May in 1939, they had no children.

His elder brother Arthur Victor was born on the 4th August 1912 in Frizinghall and also joined the RAF. Both brothers trained as navigators in Canada. Arthur flew in Lancasters and was in 49 Squdron for part of his wartime service. He was awarded the Distinguished Flying Cross in 1944. He survived two full tours of 30 missions each and retired from the RAF in 1957. He died in 1999. Arthur had married Amy Logan in 1937 and they had a daughter, she has been traced and informed of all that we have discovered of both her uncle's and father's RAF careers.

Their younger brother Leonard, born in early 1919 also served in WW2. He joined the 2nd Royal Gloucestershire Hussars which used the American M3 Stuart light tanks in North Africa. He was taken prisoner and died on the 23rd January 1942 of the wounds he had received in the Battle of Gazala. He was aged just 22 and had never married.

They had a sister Ruth, born on the 3rd of March 1917. She married Thomas Cyril Jordan in 1944. Her descendants have been traced and informed also.

Edward went on nine operations.

**Flight Sergeant Alastair Macnab McKelvie** 971310, wireless operator / gunner

Alastair McNab McKelvie was born in 1907 in Cowdenbeath, son of George McKelvie and Janet Shearer (née McNab). He married Elizabeth Walker Hume in 1929 in North Berwick and they had two children, Janet Hume McKelvie born in 1930 and Alastair Hugh George McKelvie born in 1931.

He enlisted in 1939 and had previously served in 144 Squadron where he flew in the smaller Hampden bombers for some time and earned a Distinguished Flying Medal. The citation for this reads 'For conspicuous gallantry and devotion to duty during raids into enemy territory. This N.C.O.'s work both in the air and on the ground has never left anything to be desired. The majority of his flights have been during the winter months and he has shown great skill in the working of the set under most adverse conditions. His determination and enthusiasm have had an excellent effect on the other Wireless Operator/Air Gunners in this Squadron.'

He was credited with having shot down a German Night Fighter.

McKelvie took part in nine operations with 61 Squadron and 15 on his previous tour of duty with 144 Squadron.

Surviving family members have been traced and informed of our findings.

**Sergeant Oliver Percy Beswick** 1162656, second wireless operator / gunner

Born on 21st February 1915 in Aston the son of Ernest John Beswick and Amy Bertha (née Marlow). Oliver married Dorothy Irene Thomas in early 1940. They had no children.

He had a brother, Ernest James who married but had no children and died in 1989. He also had a sister Elsie who was born in 1919 in Kings Norton. She married John Weaver in 1935. Their family has been traced and informed.

He had only done two previous missions, both with this crew.

**Flight Sergeant Norman Rhodes Hartley** 935693, Mid-upper Gunner

He was born on the 17th of October 1914 in Dublin, the son of Norman and Frances (née Mackay). He was survived by his elder sister Joan, whose descendants have also been traced and informed.

He too died on his third mission, all flown with this crew.

**Sergeant William Richard Griffiths** 1212794 Rear Gunner

My intention with this and the other appendices is to provide at least a brief biography of all of the people William met or was otherwise connected to during his adventures. I have not provided much detail for any of those whose stories are already well known and often told. Rather it is to convey my admiration and respect for the 'everyday' hero that so often passes unnoticed. That surely includes all of these brave folk.

# Appendix II

## The Aircraft

There are no records available of the aircraft that William flew in during any of his time when he was training, either in his basic gunnery training, his period on 25 Operational Training Unit or the familiarization and conversion training flights while in 61 Squadron. In October right through to January 1942 all of the Manchesters were used in the squadron's conversion training. This was often interrupted by modifications to the aircraft, the engines, cooling systems and hydraulics being modified on several occasions.

We do, however, know the identities of the seven aircraft in which he flew operational missions. This appendix is a brief description of their 70 operational sorties, and is a tribute to the airmen who served in them. Far too many of whom never came home.

All RAF aircraft had two identities. The Serial Number was always unique to the one airframe and stayed with it for its entire life. No Serial Numbers were ever reused. The Call Sign was made up from the two letter Squadron Code (QR for 61 Squadron and VN for 50 Squadron) and a single letter unique for the airplane at the time. When an aircraft was lost on operations, transferred, crashed and was written off as beyond repair then its Call Sign could be reused by a replacement aircraft. There have been many QR-Vs over the years of many different types, but only ever one L7471 which flew as QR-V with 61 Squadron and later as VN-B with 50 Squadron.

**Manchester L7471 QR-V**

Manufactured in August 1941 with triple fins and the long span (33 Foot) tail plane. Fitted with standard 3 turret armament. It may have been modified to twin fin Mk 1A standard before delivery. First issued to 61 Squadron on 9th November 1941. Transferred on the 19th April 1942 from 61 Squadron, when they were converting to Lancasters, to 50 Squadron where its new call sign was VN-B. It flew on a total of 16 operations.

On the 24th February of Flight Lieutenant McNaughton and his crew took off at 18:40 to go gardening off Wangerooge, the most easterly of the Frisian Islands. They completed the task encountering no opposition and returned safely at one minute past midnight.

Flight Lieutenant McNaughton again took L7471 for an attack on the Gneisenau at Kiel taking off at 18:00 on the 27th of February. They encountered enemy fighters on two occasions, but no attacks ensued. They returned with the tail turret and hydraulics not working after seven and a half hours.

Pilot Officer Gunter took off on a mission to bomb the Krupps works in Essen on the 9th of March at 01:40. They encountered some opposition over the target area but returned safely after eight and a half hours.

On the 10th March Flight Lieutenant McNaughton went to attack Essen taking off at 20:00. They returned at 01:20. The trip was unremarkable.

On the evening of the 13th of March Flight Lieutenant McNaughton again took L7471, this time to Cologne. They took off at 20:00 and returned after five and a half hours, another uneventful trip.

Flight Lieutenant McNaughton returned to Essen on the 25th of March. Not much opposition was reported, the flight lasted six and a quarter hours.

Flight Lieutenant McNaughton took off on the 1st of April at 19:40 to lay mines in the area off the Garonne estuary. The aircraft was picked up by searchlights near St Nazaire which McNaughton reported that he 'avoided by using I.F.F.' (IFF stood for 'Indicator Friend or Foe'. The system automatically transmitted coded signals that identified the aircraft as being British to help spot German aircraft who would not know the correct codes while in Allied airspace. There was a common misconception among bomber crews that switching on the aircraft's IFF system interfered with the German radar used to guide some searchlights. It had no such effect, though the RAF chose not to try to set the record straight for 'morale purposes'.) On the return trip they were approached on three occasions by Ju88 night-fighters but managed to avoid combat with all of these.

On the 5th of April Sergeant T A Stewart went to Cologne. Cloud and ground haze prevented precise bombing but they released their bombs and returned home.

The 8th of April was when our crew took part in the raid on the Blomm & Voss shipyard in Hamburg; this is recounted in Chapter 13,

On the 10th of April Flight Sergeant Underwood took L7471 for its last operational flight for 61 Squadron. He took off at 22:30 on a mission to bomb Essen. One engine began intermittently cutting out soon after takeoff so the bombs were jettisoned safe over the sea and he elected to land at the nearest base which was Coltishall. The engine finally quit entirely on the approach, but they landed successfully.

The next operational flight of L7471 (now with the call sign VN-B) was on the night of 16/17th May by Pilot Officer Southgate of 50 Squadron. They took off just before midnight to go gardening in the Heligoland Bight near Pellworm and Westerhever. They encountered no problems.

Flight Sergeant E J Morgan took off to bomb Mannhiem on the night of 19/20th of May. Heavy cloud covered the primary target so the bombs were dropped on the alternate target in the same town.

Sergeant A Weber took part in a mission to bomb Cologne on the night of 30/31st of May. Crossing the Dutch coast the intercom system failed, so being unable to communicate with the Air Gunners he returned to base. On the return journey the aircraft suffered from heavy tail buffeting, a not uncommon problem with the Manchester that was never completely resolved.

On the 1/2nd of June Sergeant A Weber took off to bomb Essen. He dropped his bombs on target and reported remarkably little opposition.

Sergeant Weber set out again on the night of 3/4th of June this time to Bremen. He reported that his bombs were close to the target area, but the marker flares were some way off to the north.

On the night of 5/6th June L7471 made its final flight. It took off from Skellingthorpe on a mission to bomb Emden Harbour at 23:16 flown by Flying Officer Beatty. The official report mentions that a brief SOS was heard at 01:40 but there was no further contact. Since five members of the crew survived the war we do have their accounts to piece together the events of that night.

Immediately after dropping their bomb load and turning for home the starboard engine failed. The propeller proved very difficult to feather and with the extra drag from this they lost a great deal of height coming down very close to sea level.

When the engine was finally feathered they managed to slowly climb a few hundred feet, but the strain on the remaining port engine running at maximum power proved too much. It too failed. They were forced to ditch into the sea not far from the Frisian Islands. Just another one of the many Manchesters lost entirely due to mechanical failure.

The Second Pilot, Sergeant Ronald Garnet Burton did not manage to escape from the aircraft when it hit the sea nose first. Sergeant Burton was born in 1919 the son of William and Ann Clara Frances Bidwill, of Millthorpe, New South Wales, Australia.

The rest were picked up by a German seaplane and became prisoners of war. The pilot, Flying Officer Beatty, died whilst in captivity on either the 10th or the 26th of September. Reports also differ as to whether this was from meningitis or as a result of his injuries sustained in the crash.

He is buried in Sage War Cemetery. He was the son of James Curry Beatty and Susannah Georgina Gorman Bourke, of Chatswood, New South Wales, Australia and was born in 1920. The rest of this all Australian crew survived the war and were repatriated.

The other five members of the crew were:-

Navigator - Pilot Officer Frederick William Robert Allen

First Wireless Operator & Air Gunner - Sergeant Ronald Gibson Buchanan

174

Second Wireless Operator & Air Gunner - Sergeant Alan Frederick Scanlan

Air Gunner - Sergeant Ronald Frank Davies

Air Gunner Sergeant Arthur Cambell Tebbutt

## Manchester IA L7497

Manufactured with the long span tail plane and twin fins. Fitted with standard 3 turret armament. Delivered to 61 Squadron on the 10th of October 1941. It was used on eight operations.

This aircraft took off for its first operational mission from Woolfox Lodge at 17:25 on the 10th of January 1942 to attack Emden flown by Flight Sergeant Noble. On the way to the target he was obliged to shut down the port engine due to very high oil temperature.

Typically the aircraft could not maintain height on just the starboard engine. Noble immediately set a course for home via Terschelling in the Frisian Islands where he dropped his bombs on the seaplane base there. By this time he was down to 5000 feet, but with the aircraft now much lighter managed to reach home.

On the 25th of January Flight Lieutenant Page took off at 17:50 on a mission to attack the battle cruisers Scharnhorst and Gneisenau in port at Brest. He took over half an hour flying above the area before he could identify the ships through the dense smokescreen. The Rear Gunner (Sergeant Jones) was wounded and the rear turret put out of action by the intense and accurate heavy flack during the bomb run. They returned home landing after 9 hours and 20 minutes.

Flight Sergeant Noble set off on the 14th of February at 18:20 to bomb Mannheim. They had great difficulty pinpointing the target due to dense low cloud and the snow obscuring ground features. Eventually they obtained an accurate fix on their position 30 miles from the target and made a dead reckoning approach. They bombed an area of heavy concentrated flack while the aircraft was held by intense searchlights.

The night of 24/25th of February was our crew's first operational trip to drop leaflets over Paris, detailed in Chapter 13.

On the 3rd of March Flight Sergeant Noble and his crew took their part in a raid on the Renault works in Paris flying in L7497. To try to minimise damage outside of the target area the attacks were made from low level, Noble reported his bombs exploded within the allocated target. He dropped leaflets before turning for home. He reported light flak on the return leg of the journey.

At 01:15 on the morning of the 8th of March Flying Officer Archibald took off on a mission to bomb the Krupps Works in Essen. He reported that his bombs were on target and that the flak was both heavy and accurate over the target area.

On the evening of the 10th of March Flying Officer Archibald and L7497 were once again on their way to Essen. On the return leg through Holland, which was made at very low altitude, the Air Gunners shot out several German searchlights.

At 21:10 on the 25th March 1942 Sergeant Furby took L7497 on its eighth operational flight on a mission to bomb Essen. It was shot down by Oblt Helmut Woltersdorf, NJG1 and crashed at Wertherbruch, near the Dutch/ German border.

None of the crew survived and they are all buried together in Reichswald Forest War Cemetery in the Nordrhein-Westfalen region of Germany.

Pilot - Sergeant Christopher George Furby He was the son of George Christopher Furby and Clara Florence Jackson.

Second Pilot - Flight Sergeant James Robert Dow (RCAF) He was the son of Daniel L. and Nellie J. Dow, of St. Stephen, New Brunswick, Canada.

Navigator - Sergeant John Eric Smart The son of George William Smart and Ellen Maud Button of Islington.

First Wireless Operator & Air Gunner - Sergeant Donald Charles Brockley The son of Ernest Broadway Brockley and Mary Clegg from Northwich.

Second Wireless Operator & Air Gunner - Sergeant Jack Buckley He was the son of John Albert and Mary Elizabeth Buckley, of Rochdale, Lancashire.

Air Gunner - Sergeant William Arthur Roberts The son of William Arnold Roberts and Alice Rounce of Norwich. He married Olive Agnes Trett in 1941. Their son was born in mid 1942.

Air Gunner - Sergeant Hugh Henry Featherstone He was the son of Henry and Mary Featherston; husband of Ena Featherston, of Hayes, Middlesex.

## Manchester IA L7516 QR-F

Manufactured with the long span tail plane and twin fins. Fitted with standard 3 turret armament. Delivered to 61 Squadron on the 10th of October 1941 and passed on to 50 Squadron on the 14th of April 1942 when its call sign changed. It flew on a total of 18 operations.

Squadron Leader West led the attack on the battle cruisers Scharnhorst and Gneisenau in port at Brest on the 25/26th of January 1942. They took off at 17:35 and dropped the bombs through the dense smokescreen. They were airborne just under nine hours.

The night of 31st January-1st February was Flight Sergeant Nobles' turn to take L7516 to bomb the German Battle Cruisers at Brest. He took off from Woolfox Lodge at 17:55 and landed back at North Luffenham 30 minutes after midnight with no hydraulic brake pressure.

He had bypassed Brest on the seaward side and made a direct attack from the south and released his bombs in a glide approach at 7000 feet. The bomb release mechanism malfunctioned and the bombs did not drop. When he opened the engines up to make his way clear of the target he encountered intense and accurate anti-aircraft fire. A long and dangerous trip thwarted by another mechanical failure of the Manchester aircraft.

On the 6th of February Flying Officer Beard went Gardening off Terschelling. They took off at 11:00 at returned at 14:45. The trip was uneventful. There followed an intense campaign of mine laying to cover the course that the Scharnhorst, Gneisenau and Prinz Eugen were expected to take to their North Sea ports. Manchesters were heavily involved it that exercise and 61 Squadron played its part.

Pilot Officer Smith went Gardening on the night of 16/17th of February, again off Terschelling. Although their trip was uneventful, of the two other aircraft engaged on the same task one, L7433 flown by Flight Sergeant Webster, failed to return. The other, L7473 flown by Flight Sergeant Underwood, experienced severe icing. With the extra weight the Manchester could not maintain height, and the mines had to be jettisoned. He landed at Debden, which was the nearest airfield after he crossed the English coast. Mine laying was not without its risks.

On the evening of the 21st of February two Manchesters, L7458 flown by Pilot Officer Searby and L7516 flown by Flying Officer Archibald, were sent to lay mines in the mouth of the Wesser between Wilhelmshaven and Bremerhaven. Searby, who had taken off first at 20:05, experienced severe icing in the low cloud and both aircraft were ordered to return to base.

On the 24th of February Flying Officer Archibald in L7516 was one of seven 61 Squadron Manchesters detailed to lay mines in the Heligoland Bight and Treschelling area. He took off at 18:45 in the evening. As he was crossing the Norfolk coast he was fired on by British anti-aircraft guns, he fired the correct colour Very cartridge for the day to identify his aircraft as friendly, but the firing continued.

The rest of the trip was uneventful. Of the other six Manchesters engaged in this operation three more were similarly fired upon by their own side.

L7521 flown by Flight Sergeant Underwood also came under fire from a small convoy. They did not cease fire when shown the correct colours. Pilot officer Smith in L7480 was fired on by armed trawlers escorting a small convoy, possibly the same one, with a similar lack of effect achieved by firing the colour of the day. Once in the target area he was also fired upon by the German defenders, but their barrage was much more intense and accurate. He did manage to drop his mines in the designated area.

Pilot Officer Searby flying L7518 was also fired on by a small British convoy; this may well have been a different one as they ceased fire when he fired his indentifying Very cartridges. However, when he reached his target area he found four German warships at anchor close by. Their anti-aircraft fire made life thoroughly unpleasant until he had dropped his mines and left the area.

Pilot Officer Tofield in L7464 only came under fire from the Germans, unfortunately that was so accurate that after five attempts he was unable to leave his mines behind and had to bring them home. Just two crews, Flight Lieutenant McNaughton in L7471 and Pilot Officer Hubbard in L7473, had uneventful trips. On this same night our crew was dropping leaflets over Paris on their first mission.

In the afternoon of the 27th of February Flying Officer Archibald took L7516 off from Wollfax Lodge at 17:45 to attack the Gneisenau in Kiel harbour. He had to climb to 11500 feet through thick cloud over the Danish coast, and in doing so experienced severe icing. The pitot tube also iced up and this prevented the Airspeed Indicator from working. The aircraft was repeatedly stalling and losing height while Archibald struggled to regain control. They were down to just 800 feet when they broke through the base of the cloud, though it was still too murky to establish their position.

They had no option but to set a course for home and jettison the bombs over the sea. Of the eight Manchesters from 61 Squadron taking part in this raid only three dropped their bombs over the target area, but no-one actually saw the Gneisenau.

On the 3rd of March L7516 flown by Flight Lieutenant Gascoyne-Cecil took part in the same raid on the Renault works as Flight Sergeant Noble whose experiences on this raid in L7497 have been mentioned above. L7516 took off at 19:30 and dropped leaflets and bombs from 4000 feet. The aircraft was fired on by an unidentified twin engined aircraft and the tail gunner, Flight Sergeant Say, returned fire as it closed from 150 yards until it turned away at about 50 yards range. It was not seen again, and they returned home.

On the evening of the 10th of March Pilot Officer R E Clark and our crew went to bomb the Krupps works in Essen. Their trip is recounted in Chapter 13.

Flight Sergeant Williams took off at 21:05 on the night of the 25th of March to bomb Essen. At 9,000 feet crossing the Dutch German border the rear door blew off and the intercom to the rear turret ceased working. The report does not elaborate as to why this happened. With no effective rear observation Williams decided to return, and dropped the bombs onto the Emmerich to Wesel railway line on the way home.

On the 28th of March Flight Sergeant Williams again took L7516, this time taking off at 23:45 on a mission to bomb Lubec. Being among the later aircraft to arrive at the target he reported extensive fires already burning. On the return leg of the trip he observed a large aircraft shot down over Heligoland.

On the evening of the 1st of April Flight Sergeant Williams and his crew were sent to lay mines in the area of the Garonne estuary. After only an hour's flying time they discovered that they were 15 miles off track. Unable to trust the compass, or verify their position due to the cloud cover, they returned home with the mines.

Flight Sergeant Williams had another frustrating flight in L7516 on the night of the 5th of April. Due take part in a raid on Cologne his aircraft was unable to leave its dispersal bay as the Manchester aircraft in front had strayed off the taxiway and bogged down in the soft ground. He finally took off at 02:00, but was soon recalled as he would have still been over occupied territory long after daybreak.

The Manchester was again flown by Flight Sergeant Williams on the 6th of April. They took off at 00:40 to attack the Krupps works in Essen. He dropped his bombs from 12,000 feet but was unable to positively identify the target. Some icing of the aircraft made the return trip slightly difficult, but they landed safely at 06:00. This was the last operational sortie for L7516 before it was transferred to 50 Squadron.

For its first sortie in 50 Squadron on the evening of the 15th of April Pilot Officer Goldsmith took off from Skellingthorpe in L7516 to lay mines between Belle Ile en Mer and Ile de Noirmoutier covering the approaches to St Nazaire. A seven hour round trip, the only event was that a flare briefly illuminated the aircraft, but no enemy action ensued.

At 22:30 on the evening of the 24th of April Flight Sergeant Willett set out to bomb the Heinkel Aircraft factory in Rostock. The target was clearly identified being close to the waterway, and the bombs were dropped from 3,500 feet. The bomb bay doors were damaged by light calibre flak.

On the evening of the 26th of April Flight Sergeant Willett again took off to bomb the Heinkel Aircraft factory in Rostock. This time he flew in at 5,000 and suffered from intense light calibre flak. The release mechanism failed to operate on one of the bombs.

Flight Sergeant Willett took off from Skellingthorpe at 21:42 on the 29th of April 1942 as part of a sortie to lay mines near the Frisian Islands, in an area codenamed Forgetmenot in the mouth of the Kiel Canal. They were shot down by Bf110 night-fighter flown by Oblt Gunter Kuberich of 11./NJG3 and made a forced landing on tidal mudflats near Rantum in Sylt. The events of this sortie are covered in several works including Avro Manchester: The Legend Behind the Lancaster by Robert Kirby, which gives a much fuller account of the story.

They had planted their 'Vegatables' and were returning over the Danish coast, the pilot, Willett, had climbed to 10,000 feet to give them a larger safety factor in case of engine troubles when Hannah said that he thought one of the mines had not fallen clear and was 'hung up'. He went to the forward end of the bomb bay while McDonald shone a torch through the rear observation port.

While they were doing this the Bf110 opened fire scoring hits along the whole of the rear fuselage. MacDonald went to check on the rear gunner, Williams, but it was clear from his lack of response and the extent of the damage to the aircraft that he was already dead. This was when the follow up attack occurred, and this time the Manchester's fate was sealed. Both engines were now set on fire and the wing fuel tanks leaking badly. With the Manchester steeply banked over taking what evading action Willett could still perform the upper gunner, Miners, managed to get a good burst of fire down into the cockpit area of the Messerschmitt and it broke off the attack.

Now Willett, knowing that they had lost much of the height that they had gained and believing them to be over land, gave the order to bale out. Scott and Packard quickly got the escape hatch in the aircraft's floor open, and Scott jumped through. Packard was now sat on the edge of the hatch when Willett cancelled the abandon order as he could now see that they were both too low and over water.

Ditching would now be their only option. But this did not go well, the water was far too shallow and they came to a sudden, violent halt on a sandbank. Packard was trapped half way out of the lower hatch with his legs folded back under the belly of the Manchester.

The four able bodied crew members all exited through the top escape hatch and gathered on one wing as far from the flames as possible. They were considering their very precarious position and how to rescue Packard. Both engines were still ablaze, fuel was leaking from the damaged tanks, there were fires quite close to large amounts of ammunition and the remaining mine hung up in the bomb bay could explode at any moment.

Suddenly Packard was seen struggling on the surface of the water near the wing. He had somehow managed to get himself free. They pulled him up onto the wing, barely alive and with badly injured legs. The five men decided it would be better to try to wade to shore, but it was hard going in the dark while also supporting the injured Packard. They found that the shallow water over the sandbanks was criss-crossed with deeper tidal channels, and in one of these they discovered Scott's body floating in the water. His Mae West was inflated, but his parachute was missing.

They eventually had no other option than to return to the

aircraft. They were picked up not long afterwards by some German troops using a small inflatable boat. Later they learned that in the second pass that the Bf110 made on the Manchester, the Mid-upper gunner, Miners, had killed the German rear gunner and badly damaged the night fighter.

That was not quite the end of this tale. The Germans knew that the unexploded mine still hung up in the Manchester was of a new type designed to be difficult to 'sweep', and would be well worth recovering. While they were attempting to remove it on the day after the crash, the thing exploded. All of the recovery party were killed and the mine kept its secrets a little longer.

The crew were:-

Pilot - Flight Sergeant Stanley Willett DFM who became a Prisoner of War.

2nd Pilot - Flight Sergeant S E Packard Also became a Prisoner of War.

Navigator - Pilot Officer Neil Hannah Also became a Prisoner of War.

1st Wireless Operator - Flight Sergeant Hector S. McDonald Also a Prisoner of War confined in hospital due to severe injuries to one hand. He was repatriated in October 1943.

2nd Wireless Operator - Sergeant Clarence Alfred Miners RAAF Also became a Prisoner of War.

Air Gunner - Sergeant David Alexander Williams died in the initial attack. He was the son of Vivian Vasey Woodthorpe Williams and Dorothy Maybury Williams, of Wahroonga, New South Wales, Australia. He is buried in Kiel War

Cemetery.

Air Gunner - Cecil John Scott was the only one to have escaped from the aircraft before it ditched. It is not clear whether he drowned or was killed when his parachute detached itself. It is possible that he may even have left the aircraft without it. He was the son of William Frank Scott and Elsie Kate Snook of Amesbury and is buried in Kiel War Cemetery.

## Manchester R5786 QR-E

Part of a somewhat mixed batch, some were completed as MK IAs with the enlarged 'Lancaster sized' twin fins, no central fin and the long span tailplane, but this one was delivered to 61 Squadron on the 10th of October 1941 in Mk I configuration with the smaller twin fins and the central fin, It had the standard three turret defensive armament and completed ten operations. It was the only one of the seven aircraft listed in this appendix not to have been lost on an operation.

On the 9th of March Pilot Officer Clark and his crew laid mines off the French coast near Lorient, although they were fired on by very heavy flack, there was no serious damage done to the aircraft. The six hour trip was otherwise uneventful. William did not go with his crew on this occasion, his place in the rear turret being taken by a Sergeant Hanson who was usually part of Seibold's crew.

On the 23rd of March Pilot Officer Seibold and crew made a five hour sortie to lay mines. They landed at Exeter due to poor weather at their home station, but reported nothing else of interest.

Pilot Officer Clark and our crew had engine troubles when

taking part in a raid on Lubeck on the night of 28/29th March. This is recounted in detail in Chapter 13.

On the 1st of April Pilot Turner took his crew to drop leaflets over Paris. The trip was uneventful although the weather was bad.

Pilot Officer Seibold flew on a mission to bomb Cologne on the 5th of April. He managed to evade a night fighter just before reaching the target. Then the hydraulics failed and they had a struggle to get the bomb doors open. By this time they had over flown their allocated target by some considerable distance and released their bombs over the first town they saw, probably Bonn. The return trip had to be made with the bomb doors open, with the extra drag taking its toll of the engines and the fuel consumption. Concerned also about the state of the hydraulics he elected to land at Feltwell in Norfolk.

Soon after this last operation R5786 was transferred to 50 Squadron operating out of Skellingthorpe with most of the other 61 Squadron Manchesters.

On the night of 19/20th April Pilot Officer Goldsmith and his crew went on a Gardening expedition to Terschelling in R5786. The trip was entirely uneventful.

Pilot Officer Goldsmith took part in the same bombing raid on the Heinkel factory at Rostock as Flight Sergeant Willett in L7516. Goldsmith had another uneventful trip of just short of eight hours.

On the 29/30th of the same month Sergeant Gruber took R5786 out Gardening to Langeland. A six and a half hour trip, also uneventful.

Flying Officer Stone and crew took a trip to Avranches & Rennes to drop leaflets on the night of 2/3rd of May. An uneventful flight of six hours.

Things were not so uneventful on the night of the 19/20th of May. Sergeant Gray was detailed on a mission to Le Mans and took off just after 22:00. The aircraft had some issues, aborted the mission and returned three hours later. There are no details as to the problems they encountered, and the two reports of the mission in the squadron records also differ. The Operation Record Book details list it as a bombing mission, but the Summary has it as a leaflet drop, the later is more likely. This was to be R5686's last operational mission.

On the night of the 29/30th of May Pilot Officer Garland was involved in one of two squadron 50 Manchester crashes. Both crews were undertaking their conversion training when the weather turned against them. L7492 with Sergeant Eyres at the controls suffered a radio failure and returned to Skellingthorpe. The local Air Traffic control could not warn him that the poor visibility and heavy rain had made landing there very risky.

He flared for his landing while still too high, and came down heavily on one main wheel causing the undercarriage to collapse. With the runway blocked Garland, in R5786, was diverted to land at Waddington. He too misjudged his approach at an unfamiliar airfield and in the bad weather.

The Manchester touched down too far along the grass runway. With the wet grass and insufficient runway he could not slow down in time and crashed through the airfield boundary fence, across a country road and the Manchester slid down a small embankment into a field. The aircraft was badly damaged and two crew members injured.

Although R5786 was repaired by 3rd June it took part in no more operational flights. It was transferred to 164 Heavy Conversion Unit on the 18th of July and was finally scrapped on the 28th of January 1943 after another crash landing caused by engine failure.

## Lancaster R5613 QR-B

On the night of 29/30th May 1942 Flying Officer G L Tofield took off on a Gardening mission just off the Danish Coast. The primary area had too much low cloud cover and they planted their vegetables in the alternative area near Fano. The trip of four and a half hours was otherwise unremarkable.

Flight Lieutenant P R Casement took his part in the 1000 bomber raid to Cologne on the night of the 30/31st of May. Their mission was successfully completed without incident.

Casement went to Essen on the night of 1/2nd June and bombed the railway sidings. Returning home he was over the Dutch coast when they were intercepted by two Bf109s. He executed some violent manoeuvres and the German aircraft turned their attention to a slower Wellington bomber on a parallel course nearby.

The night of 2/3rd of June was when this aircraft met its end over Belgium with our crew onboard. It was only its fourth operational sortie.

## Lancaster R5615 QR-H

On the night of 22/23rd of May Squadron Leader P W M West went Gardening near Swinemunde. One of the Gunners, Pilot Officer R W Kominski, reported that he had fired on a Heinkel He113 night fighter that they crossed paths with.

There never was a He113 night fighter. It was all a disinformation campaign by the German military. It was much publicised version of the He100 fighter which held the then current World Speed Record at over 394MPH. Even the He100 never actually entered service with the Luftwaffe. Nevertheless many allied airmen reported encounters with both of these types. The very few examples that were built had been much photographed in many different squadron markings. Their outlines were very similar to the Bf109.

Pilot Officer Clark and our crew took part in the same Gardening mission as Tofield in R5613 on the night of 29/30th May, which is listed above. Our crew's trip is detailed in Chapter 13.

On the 30/31st May Flight Sergeant G E Williams took the Lancaster on the 1000 bomber raid to Cologne. Their trip was uneventful.

Flight Sergeant Williams flew the Lancaster again on the night of 1/2nd June, this time to Essen. Another quiet trip.

On the night of 3/4th June Flight Sergeant Williams took off and bombed Bremen. Nothing unusual to report.

When Flight Sergeant N R Meyer set out for Emden on the night of 6/7th June the Air Speed Indicator failed while they were over the North Sea. Meyer jettisoned the bombs and returned early to Syerston.

On the night of 7/8th of June Flight Sergeant Williams went mine laying off the coast near Terschelling. He reported a Flak ship just to the south of his target area.

Flight Sergeant Meyer set out on the night of 16/17th of June to bomb Essen. His TR1335 navigational aid (Gee) failed in the target area, and with solid cloud cover he turned for home. Over the German airfield near Naarmsesteen, with his Gee now working again, he dropped his bombs.

On the night of 18/19 June Flight Sergeant Williams went Gardening in the area of Schiermonnikoog and Terschelling. Having laid the mines he exchanged fire with a Flak ship in the vicinity.

Flight Sergeant Williams set out at 23:45 on 22nd of June for an attack on Emden. On the return over the North Sea they dropped to 100 feet to check two lights on the water surface. They could not make out what they were and returned to base.

On the night of 25/26th June Flight Sergeant Williams took part in a bombing raid to the Focke-Wulf aircraft works in Bremen. The trip was uneventful.

Flight Sergeant Gregory took off at 23:30 on the night of 27th of June 1942 for an operation to Bremen. The aircraft was hit by heavy Flak and crashed at around 01:30 the following morning. None of the crew survived and all seven are buried together in Becklingen War Cemetery, Niedersachsen, Germany. This was the Lancaster's 12th operational flight.

The crew were:-

Pilot Flight Sergeant Paul Walter Gregory - Son of Percy Walter James Gregory and Dorothy Bessie Ellis, of Paignton, Devon.

2nd Pilot Sergeant James Henry Kinch RCAF - Born in 1914 the son of John Peter Kinch and Wynogene Jane Wellington of Ontario.

Navigator Pilot Officer William James Ruddy RCAF - Born in 1917 the son of Albert James Ruddy and Hazel Madeline Loney, of Windsor, Ontario, Canada. He had married Phyllis Rae Parsons in April 1939 in Toronto, they had no children.

Wireless Operator/Air Gunner Flight Sergeant Frank Roe Born in 1918 the son of Alfred Roe and Gertrude Fowler, of Hessle, Yorkshire. He had only recently married Mary Doreen Cook.

Wireless Operator/Air Gunner Sergeant Harold Dauncey - Born in 1919 the son of Herbert Griffin Dauncey and Alice Breese, of Birmingham.

1st Air Gunner Sergeant John Grocock Born in 1919 the son of John Percy Grocock and Ida May Muddiman, of Doncaster, Yorkshire.

2nd Air Gunner Sergeant Edmund Robert John Burrell 19 years old, the son of Robert Burrell and Marion Lily Burrell, of Colchester, Essex.

**Lancaster R5627 QR-L**

On the night of 30/31st May Pilot Officer R E Clark and our crew took their part in the first 1000 bomber raid on Cologne. Their experience has already been told in Chapter 13.

At 22:50 on the night of 1st of June Flying Officer Archibald took off on a mission to bomb Essen. Over the target area one engine cut out, but they returned safely to base.

On the 3rd of June Flying Officer Archibald flew R5627 on its third operational mission. They took off from RAF Syerston at 23:15 to go to Bremen. At around 01:30 near Oldenburg the Lancaster was shot down by a Bf110 flown by

Hans-Heinrich König of 8./NJG3 and crashed near Bad Zwischenahn aerodrome. There was just the one survivor, the rest of the crew were interred locally and later reburied in Sage War Cemetery.

The crew were:-

Pilot Flying Officer Ronald Earle Archibald. Son of Wilbert Earle Archibald and Clara Jennie Petersen, of Rosedale, British Columbia, Canada. He was born in Chilliwack in September 1920. He joined the RAF in 1939 and was posted to operation flying with Bomber Command in September 1941.

2nd Pilot Sergeant Peter Holmes survived to become a prisoner of war and was subsequently liberated and repatriated.

Navigator Flight Sergeant Ian Frank Pratt. The son of Frank Percy Pratt and Olive Goode, of Margaretting, Essex. He was born at the end of 1920.

1st Wireless Operator Flight Sergeant David Lorimer D.F.M. Just 20 years old, from Broughty Ferry in the Dundee area the son of Mr David Lorimer and Alexina Smart. He had married Irene Merrill of Leicester on the 2nd of April 1942 in Broughty Ferry.

2nd Wireless Operator Sergeant Jack Lewis Wallis. Born in 1912, the son of Charles Wallis and Florence Ward, of Wood Green, Middlesex, England.

1st Air Gunner Flight Lieutenant George Liddell Carruthers Beattie Born in 1902 the son of Sir J Carruthers Beattie of Cape Town. He had married Winifrede Jean Laird in 1931 in Marylebone, they had no children.

2nd Air Gunner Flight Sergeant Maurice Hamilton Denison. Born in 1906 the son of George Ellis Denison and Katherine Myfanwy Jones. He married Lucy Mary Alice Featherstone of Fixby in 1940.

# Appendix III

# The Comète Line Members

It is not my intention to provide a complete story of the Comète Line here. There are many excellent books that do just that, and several more that include the Comète Line in their coverage of escape and evasion from occupied Europe. My intention is to honour those brave souls who personally assisted William Griffiths in his return to Britain, particularly those who are not mentioned in any of those works. These are listed in order of their appearance in the account of his escape.

### Jean Maurice De Praetere (Delbo)

He was born in 1919 in Woluwé-St-Pierre. In 1940 he was a Sergeant in the 2nd Lancers of the Belgian Army having joined up in 1938. When he helped William on the morning of the 3rd of June 1942 he was already planning his journey to England to continue his fight for his homeland.

Jean left for Paris with Elvire Morelle and Harold Edison De Mone on the 8th of June. De Mone was the gunner in a Wellington bomber shot down returning from a mission to Essen on the night of 1/2nd of June. The two stayed a few days with René and Raymonde Coache where they met Horsley and Baveystock. These two were in  the same Manchester bomber from 50 Squadron that was hit by flak while taking part in the 1000 bomber raid on Cologne on the night of 30/31st May 1942. Three other members of that crew also managed to evade capture and return to Britain, all of their paths crossing from time to time on the journey. One other crew member, Pilot Officer R J Barnes, was captured and served out the war in Stalag Luft III.

Their pilot, Pilot Officer Leslie Thomas Manser managed to fly the crippled Manchester out of Germany to give his crew the slim hope of evading capture, and only gave the order to evacuate the plane when it became too difficult to keep in the air. It fell to earth in flames only a few moments later with Manser still at the controls. He died in the crash and was posthumously awarded the Victoria Cross.

The party left Paris on the night train for the border on the 10th of June with Dédée and on the 13th escaped over the Pyrenees. After his arrival in Britain on the 10th of August De Praetere soon started training as a secret agent, and was given the code name Delbo. He was dropped by parachute into France on the 18th of May 1943 and ran the Phoenix network until he was arrested in April 1944. He was still in Dachau when it was liberated on the 19th of June 1945. He returned to Belgium after the war and lived in Rosières.


## Jules Flament

Beyond the fact that this brave man lived in Genappe and sheltered allied airmen, so far I have been unable to find any further information.


## Dr Georges Blanpain

All that I have been able to establish so far is that he was born in January 1899 in Waterloo, survived the war and died September 1975 in Brussels. He attended to several Allied evaders.


## Joséphine Van Durme (Josée)

She was born in Waterloo in 1914, by 1939 she was a teacher. With her fiancé Jules Colle she was active in both the local Resistance and the Comète line. She was a national guide for the escape line and sheltered several escaping airmen, including our William, as well as providing clothes and food. She was also the cook and 'housekeeper' for the Resistance in Waterloo. She produced forged Identity Papers for both organisations.

In late 1943 the Resistance group was betrayed and the secretly partitioned section of a water tower that held their living quarters and armoury was raided by the Gestapo on November the 3rd. Joséphine, Jules and two others managed to escape to Brussels. She and Jules were arrested there on the 10th of the same month.

She was held in Saint-Giles prison where she suffered greatly before being sentenced to death. In May 1944 she was in a prison camp in Cottbus Germany, and later on in Waldheim. She was liberated from there on the 6th of May when the Russian army arrived, and subsequently repatriated to Waterloo.

She returned to the school where she had previously taught, eventually becoming the head of the Ecole de Saint Anne in Waterloo. She never married and never spoke about her wartime experiences. She died in December 2009 in Belgium.

## Gustave Delaide

He was born in 1904 in Waterloo. In 1942 Gustave was a farmer in the village of Le Roussart just to the east of Waterloo and an active member of the Belgian Resistance who also helped the Comète Line. He was arrested on the 3rd of November 1943 as a result of the Gestapo raid on the Water Tower hideout and had a very unpleasant stay in the former Belgian Army Fort Breendonk, which the Germans had taken over to use as in interrogation centre. On the 29th of April 1944 he was convicted for membership of the Resistance and storing arms. He was sentenced to death.

He then transferred through a series of prison camps going from Bruchsall to Brandenburg in early January 1945 and from there to Sonnenburg (now Słońsk in Poland).

On the night of the 30/31st of January with the Russian Army approaching from the west the German SS assembled the 819 prisoners who were mobile in the rear courtyard including Gustave and three other members of the same Resistance unit; Jean Barette, Alexandre Denayer and André Jadin.

The Germans systematically machine gunned them all. Only four prisoners survived until the Russians arrived just two days later. All of the rest, including the four mentioned, now lie in one of the mass graves dug by the relieving Russian soldiers at the site.

## Jules Colle (Mr Jules)

Born in 1911, he was a professor at the College Cardinal Mercier in Braine and a reserve lieutenant with the Grenadiers. He became the local leader in Waterloo Zone IV,

South Sector, Belgian Legion, Secret Army, the name for his part of the Belgian Resistance. They were using the Hotel Saint-Michel as their headquarters; this was actually leased to occupying forces at the time, but they did not use any part of the building.

Joséphine Van Durme and her sister Jeanne were the only ones that ever visited the hotel acting as cooks and housekeepers to the 'guests'. After some time the Germans informed the Hotel owner that they would soon start using the building and asked him to make sure everything was ready for them. That meant something entirely different to him. The Resistance would have to move out at very short notice.

They moved to part of the attic of an elementary school just across the courtyard. One end of this attic was the flat for the caretakers, the other end was used by the Germans to store 'confiscated' furniture and between these two was a large water storage tank. The resistance quickly erected a partition in the German storeroom and turned this space into three sections, a dormitory, living quarters and an armoury. Although the conditions were more than a little restrictive, this arrangement worked well enough, the Germans and the school users, apart from the caretakers, were completely unaware of their presence.

On the evening of the 2nd of November Jean Barette, one of members of the group, was arrested by the Nazis as the result of a careless lapse. News soon reached the rest of the group, and they immediately dismantled their hiding place, even replacing the dust from the floor that had been carefully preserved. Some members dispersed to other safe places, and Alexandre Léonard and Francois Barette went out to find a

199

truck to move all the weapons and personal possessions. However the Germans appeared before this truck arrived. The caretakers waited in the kitchen of the school while everyone else made their escapes.

Alexandre Denayer and René Menada jumped over a wall straight into a group of soldiers, Denayer was swiftly apprehended but Menada was shot while still trying to escape. Jules Colle, Joséphine Van Durme, Jules Bouquieaux and Jean Flacon also ran into a German guard. Jean Flacon, who was the only one of the entire group to have been trained as a Secret Agent in Britain, overpowered and killed the soldier while the other three made their escape.

Flacon also escaped and served out the rest of the war in Belgium, and later in Denmark, where his code name was Georges. In the midst of all of this chaos and confusion the truck turned up, fortunately the two men heard the gunfire and shouting and made their way to a safe house instead.

Jules Colle and Josephine Van Durme were arrested a week later in Brussels. As told above Joséphine survived her ordeals in the various prison camps. Jules was not so fortunate. After prolonged interrogation and torture at Breendonk he was sent to Poppenweiler camp near Ludwigsburg. He was executed there on the 30th of September 1944 with Joseph Poelaert, another member of the same Resistance group.

After the war the remains of Jules Colle and Joseph Poelaert were repatriated and buried in the old Cimetière du Centre de Waterloo which is on the Drève Dix Meters, a street perpendicular to the Avenue Jules Colle named in his honour.

## Jeanne Plettinckx

The mother of Joséphine Delbrouck who was called on to shelter escapers from time to time at her home on the Chaussée de Bruxelles.

## Dr. Antoine Goethals

I have not uncovered any information about this man, apart from the fact that he was an active member of the Comète Line, many evaders were sheltered at his home.

## Baron Albert Marie Louis Greindl

He was born on 2nd October 1914 in Brussels, and was a lawyer. He had served in the Belgian Army and was a Prisoner of War from May 1940 until August. He was one of the founder members of the Comète escape line. In February 1943 the Germans arrested many of the Comète members, including his brother Jean, and on the 12th of that month he left Brussels with Jean-François Nothomb, Bee Johnson and three evaders.

This was to be the first attempted crossing into Spain since Dédée and her entire party were arrested at Franchia's farmhouse in Ciboure, and things did not go smoothly. Having reached a safe house in Elizondo on the Spanish side of the border Nothomb went to a nearby village to fetch a taxi to take the party to San Sabastian. The taxi with Nothomb and the three airmen was stopped at a checkpoint on the way and the four were all arrested. Nothomb managed to pass himself off as an escaping French Canadian Airman.

They spent a thoroughly unpleasant few days in the prison at Pamplona. Meanwhile Johnson and Greindl took the train to San Sebastian and contacted the Vice-Consul who then collected the other four from their prison. By the 25th of February the six were reunited and on their way to Gibraltar.

Once in Britain Greindl volunteered to return to Europe to work undercover. During a parachute jump as part of his training he landed badly and broke his back. This delayed him for six weeks until he was finally out of the full body plaster cast and fit again. Since another parachute drop would have been too dangerous for him, he was flown to Gibraltar on 17th of February 1944 and was infiltrated overland into France on 11th of April.

He was arrested making another crossing of the Spanish-French border on 23rd April on his way to Perpignan, and interned there. Later he was moved to Fresnes prison, where he was tortured. He was released when the Swedish consul persuaded von Cholditz , the German officer in charge there that liberation was an imminent certainty.  He died in Ottignies-Louvain-la-Neuve in 1991.

## Octave Mondo

Born in 1897 Octave as well as working for the Comète Line he was also active in the Resistance and Rebels Silencieux who used both passive and active methods to prevent people, especially Jewish folk, from being deported to German concentration camps.

He was arrested on 1st July 1943 and shot in Luswigsburg on June 30th 1944.

## Suzanne Mondo née Watrin

Born in 1897 she too was involved in many patriotic endeavours alongside her husband. They had two children Jacqueline (born in 1923) and Walter (born in 1926).

She was detained and ended up being sent to Ravensbrück concentration camp. By early 1945 around 50,000 prisoners were still in Ravensbrück. With the Russia Army's rapid approach in the spring the SS decided to remove as many prisoners as they could, in order to avoid leaving live witnesses behind who could testify as to what had occurred in the camp. All physically capable women, about 24.500 were forced to march to northern Mecklenburg.

On 30th April 1945, fewer than 3,500 malnourished and sickly prisoners were discovered alive at the camp when it was liberated by the Red Army. The survivors of the death march were liberated soon afterwards by a Soviet scouting party. Most of these poor souls were handed over to the Swedish Red Cross.

There are conflicting accounts as to the circumstances of her death, though they agree on the date of on 29th April 1945. It seems most likely that she died in Malente on the way to Sweden while under the care of the Red Cross.


## Marguerite Eulalie Van Lier (Michèle, Melle Mitchell, Peggy)

Born on March 16th 1915 in Johannesburg South Africa her father was a Belgian trader and her mother was a South

African of Irish descent, she inherited her mother's thick red hair. She spoke fluent English, Flemish, French and German. In 1941 she was asked by Frédéric De Jongh to help to run the Comète line's operations in Belgium.

She then lived at 72 Rue de Bruxelles in Ha and worked with Jean Greindl ("Nemo") whose work running a Brussels-based Swedish Red Cross organisation provided cover for the resistance and escape line activities. In November 1942 she went to the home of Victor Michiels to warn him that he could be in imminent danger of arrest. Unfortunately the Gestapo were already there waiting for Michiels, and she was arrested.

Peggy was interrogated, but stuck to her story that she merely wanted to talk to Victor's sister and was not acquainted with Victor himself. Since she had photographs of herself with several German soldiers and spoke such good German she managed to make them believe her story and she was released. A few days later on the 6th of December she was over the border into Spain and on her way to England.

She made a good impression on James Madon Langley (he conducted almost all of the MI9 interviews with anyone who passed through the escape lines) that he got her a job at the War Office organising the transport of military VIPs. The couple married in 1943. She was later awarded an MBE. Peggy died in Lewes in 2000.


**Carl Servais**

He was born in 1903 in Louvain-la-Neuve. He was a radio operator for the local Resistance group and many Comète Line 'parcels' spent some time sheltered in his home on Rue

Stevens Delannoy. He was eventually arrested and by the latter half of 1944 he was incarcerated in Saint-Giles prison.

He was still there in September 1944 when the German authorities decided that with the fall of Brussels imminently expected all of the prisoners held in Saint-Giles would be sent to Neuengamme concentration camp in Germany. They arranged for a train to carry the 1370 'political prisoners' (mostly Belgian Resistance members, Escape line helpers and sundry others) and a further 41 allied prisoners of war.

The train of 32 goods wagons and a flat car with an anti-aircraft gun and four machine guns bringing up the rear was scheduled to leave Brussels Midi Station early in the morning of Saturday the 2nd of September. This was the now famous 'Ghost Train', and things did not quite go entirely as the Germans had expected.

At 07:30, an hour before the planned departure, the Assistant Station Manager Michel Petit, who was a member of Mouvement National Belge resistance group, had already begun the operation to thwart the German intentions. Several locomotives suddenly became unserviceable, and the rest were recalled to the central depot.

Train drivers disappeared, became too ill to work or went off having been injured in 'accidents'. By 09:15 the depot was asked to provide an engine, which of course happened to be not working, nor was the one requested later as a replacement. The Germans had to send their own engineers to oversee the repairs before they managed to secure a working locomotive. Unfortunately this was then sent to a different and remote part of the marshalling yard due to a 'misunderstanding'.

It was 16:15 before the Germans finally had an engine coupled to the train, and a crew for it. The driver and fireman would have the company of three armed German guards on the footplate at all times to make sure there would be no further delays. The driver insisted on performing a complete brake check before setting off, though in fact he used his stroll down the length of the train to inform the prisoners of the situation and collect the messages that they had managed to post out of the slats in the sides and the open vents in the wagons.

The train finally left over eight hours late, but even then it did not get far. Within five minutes it was shunted onto a dead end track at Forest-Midi station while a 72 wagon goods train was assembled on the instructions of the German authorities. While this would normally be done in the sidings there the railwaymen had convinced the Germans that this was not possible due to the length of the train and some damage to the sidings. Nor was the shunting and sorting done particularly efficiently.

After almost an hour the decision was made to send the train back north and in the process of moving the engine to the other end of the train the flatcar with the antiaircraft and machine guns somehow became detached and was left behind.

At 17:45 the train arrived at Schaerbeek railway marshalling yard and there were more delays due to signals stuck on stop, but eventually at around 23:00 they reached Mechelen where the driver, Louis Verheggen, needed to replenish the water tanks. As the driver was well aware, the water supply there was not working due to recent bombing and they had to divert the train to the very busy station at Muizen.

The guards failed to realize that the reason the engine was so low on water after less than 20 kilometres of travel was that the crew had been keeping the water drain valve slightly open the whole time. Their very fine judgement and timing made sure that the train was well setup for some more serious delays. It would not be sent out to return to Mechelen until 05:30 on Sunday morning.

On the way back to Mechelen the wheels of the engine began to slip, especially on the turns. The driver was deliberately mishandling the locomotive and also refrained from using the sand blowers. The railwaymen convinced the guards that the engine was faulty and they would have to send for a second locomotive to get them safely back to a depot for repairs.

By 10:15 they had arrived at La Petite Ile station with Gerardy driving this second engine. Meanwhile the fireman, Léon Pochet, had been a little remiss in his duties and the fire on the original engine had died right down. Verheggen, the driver, managed to make his escape while inspecting the engine to 'determine the cause of the trouble' and was briefly out of sight of the guards. Since Gerady and his engine had been immediately commandeered to haul a train full of German troops fleeing the British advance, which by this time was well into the suburbs of Brussels, the train full of prisoners would be going nowhere in a hurry.

At 10:45 with a suspected faulty locomotive with no steam pressure and no driver the future of the train came under intense discussion involving a Doctor Van Dooren (whose wife was a prisoner in one of the trucks), representatives of the Red Cross and the German officer in charge of the train. By 12:30 it was decided that all of the 'political prisoners' would be released in exchange for a driver. The train would then return to the marshalling yard at Schaerbeek still with the PoWs on board and collect as many German troops as possible and evacuate them to Germany.

At Schaerbeek there was a final brilliant example of really skilled railcraft when the train was getting ready to depart. Just as the train was slowly crossing a complex set of points the signalman 'made a slight error' in his timing and some cars at the rear of the train were gently derailed, they just happened to be the ones full of the allied prisoners of war.

Since the Germans in the rest of the train seemed quite keen to be on their way without further delay these cars were simply uncoupled and left where they were. The prisoners were finally free to do as they wished. With gunfire getting ever closer they chose to wait until daybreak by which time the liberation of Brussels was complete.

Carl Servais died in 1991.

On a personal note I have to say that I have found the appendices particularly hard to write. Not because the research for them has been difficult, though parts of it certainly have been, but in so many cases I have been able to find little information about these very courageous people, far too many of whom lost their lives, and even those who survived often paid a truly terrible price for their patriotism. They deserve to be better remembered. This last section however I have found quite rewarding.

I stand absolutely in awe of the Belgian railwaymen who coolly, calmly and without resorting to arms managed to so completely out manoeuvre the highly trained Waffen SS. I am in no doubt that had the Germans realised what was happening all around them was as a result of subterfuge rather than incompetence many of these brave citizens would have been summarily executed, and the railwaymen knew that too.

With a mix of skilled handling (actually mishandling) of the locomotives and signals, deliberate misunderstanding of instructions, feigning illness and staging accidents, and sheer breadth and depth of knowledge of how their railway system worked these couple of dozen civilians rescued over 1400 people who otherwise faced a very short and unpleasant future. I have been able to name a few in this story; I wish that I could properly honour the rest by name too.

## Count Georges Albert Ferdinand Paul Marie Ghislain d'Oultremont (Charles, Charlie Ormonde, Romeo, Laporte)

He was born in The Hague on April 4th 1916 and served in the Belgian Army from July 1939 until he was captured on the 28th of May 1940. He was released a few months later. He then began working for the Comète Line from March 1942 as a guide on the route from Brussels to Paris.

Knowing that his name had become known to both the Gestapo and the Abwehr he was evacuated by the Comète Line to England on December 6th 1942. In Britain he received training to return behind the lines.

He was taken by Lysander on the 7th of November 1943 to Compiègne. His task was to connect with the Comète Line and to shelter downed pilots in the woods in the 'Marathon' camps as it was becoming more dangerous to reach and cross the Spanish border. When many members of his group were arrested he was ordered to try to escape through Spain, but this time ended up under house arrest in Pamplona by February 1944. In March his house arrest was ended and he was back in Britain by the 4th of April. He was in Bayeux during July 1944 again assisting more people to escape from occupied Europe.

On the 28th of August 28 1944 he landed near Godinne in the Belgian Ardennes with the Belgian paratroopers led by Lieutenant-Colonel Edouard Blondeel. He was in charge of an armoured reconnaissance section and remained there until January 1945 when he entered Germany with the Allied advance.

He was awarded the Military Medal and was made a Member of the British Empire by the British government. He died in 1993.


### Andrée De Jongh (Dédée)

She was the utterly remarkable young woman who instigated the entire Comète network. As such she is the subject of many books and articles, some entirely factual and some fictionalised. Since she is so well documented elsewhere (and rightly so) this will only be a very brief outline.

Born in late 1916 she gave up her job at the outbreak of the war to join the Red Cross, where she was already training as a nurse and ambulance driver. She was captured on the 15th of January 1943 and tortured extensively in various prisons eventually ending up in Mauthausen from where she was liberated by the International Red Cross on April 22nd 1945. She completed her training as a nurse and worked in several African countries. She never married. She returned to Belgium and died there in 2007. She was presented with many awards and medals for her service during the war including the George Medal.

## Frédéric De Jongh (Paul)

Dédée's father. He was born in 1897 and was the Principle of the school in Gaucheret Street in Schaerbeek which now bears his name. He too is well documented so again this will only be a brief summary.

When his daughter suggested setting up an organised escape line for allied personnel to his eternal credit he did not even attempt to dissuade her. He knew that would have been a waste of time. He realised that the best way her could try to protect her in this dangerous venture was to help with the organisation, so he too became involved. After the line was betrayed by Jacques Desoubrie he was arrested by the Gestapo on the 7th of June 1943. He was executed by firing squad on the 3rd of March 28th 1944 at the Fortress of Mont-Valérien.

## René Marie Gustave Coache

He was born in France in 1904. His home in Asnières-sur-Seine was used as a safe house and about 30 evaders or escapers passed through it between 1941 and 1942. He left Paris on December 31st 1942 with three American airmen accompanied by Charles Gueulette, François Nothomb (Franco) and Dédée by train to Bayonne and then on to Saint-Jean-de-Luz in the afternoon.

The party crossed the Pyrenees that same night with 'Bee'

Johnson. In Britain René trained as a clandestine radio operator and parachuted to Brussels in November 15th 1943 to be the radio operator code named 'Dover' for the Comète escape line. The Gestapo arrested him on April 21th 1944 and he was incarcerated in Saint-Gilles until September 3rd 1944 when he too escaped from the 'Ghost Train' in the confusion of the German withdrawal.

## Raymonde Coache née Gouet

The wife of René Marie Gustave Coache, she was born in 1898. She fled to Lille in December 1942 when her husband left for Britain and was soon active again helping Allied airmen to evade capture. She was arrested in Lille in June 1943 as a result of the Comète line's betrayal by the infamous Jacques Desoubrie.

Raymonde survived her time in the concentration camps finally ending up in Bergan-Belsen. She returned to Paris and lived peacefully with René in their old flat near the Seine. She was awarded the MBE.

## Captain Léon Violette

Léon was born in Landry in September 1880. His home in Rue Emile Deouen in Vincennes was used as a safe house by the Comète Line in 1942. Many evaders were briefly sheltered there.

## Béatrice Violette née Crane

The wife of Léon Violette she was born in Nottingham on the 30th of April 1879.

## Elvire Morelle (Irene)

She was born in 1908 and one of the French Comète Line members. She joined the Comète Line in July 1941 and accompanied evaders from Brussels to Paris and then on to Bayonne. She also made one eventful crossing of the Pyrenees as a guide in February 1942; this is recounted in Chapter 20. She then became the cook and general housekeeper in a safe house on the outskirts of Paris which she rented. Later she rented a flat in the Rue Oudinot in the centre of Paris for the same purpose.

At that time three different apartments in that same building were being used by the Comète Line for nearly a year. The evidently patriotic concierge kept their little secret. Elvirie was arrested on the 19th of November 1942 when the Comète Line had been compromised by two Germans agents posing as evading American airmen; almost 100 people were arrested at that time. Not all of them survived. She was still at Mauthausen concentration camp when it was liberated at the end of April 1945. She lived out the rest of her peaceful life in Bidart on the French Atlantic coast between Bayonne and Saint-Jean-de-Luz. She was awarded the MBE.

## Elvire De Greef (Tante Go)

She was born in Brussels in 1897. The family, with Albert 'B' Johnson, fled to the Bayonne area in May 1940 with the intention of crossing into Spain and eventually reaching

England. Unable to do so at the time they settled in the Villa Voisin in Anglet. Her husband, Fernand, worked for the German occupiers as an interpreter in their headquarters. With his access to official documents, including blank ones, and rubber stamps combined with Elvire's connections to the black market and the local smugglers they were well set up to aid both the escape lines and resistance.

Elvire was never arrested and after the war was awarded the George Medal. She died in Brussels in 1991

## Janine De Greef

Born in Brussels in 1925 she also worked for the Comète Line. She was involved in accompanying evaders from Paris to one of the safe houses in Saint-Jean-de-Luz and from there to the remoter farmhouses where they would meet their Basque guides for the trip over the border.

In March 1944 when the Comète Line had been compromised she herself fled over the border and on to England. She returned to Brussels after the war and died there in 2020

## Albert Edward Johnson (B or Bee)

Albert was born in Farringdon, Hampshire in September 1908. From 1928 he was the driver and mechanic for the International Olympic Committee in Brussels. In May 1940 he joined the De Greef Family in their flight to Anglet. Johnson's false papers proclaimed him to be Albert Jonion, of Belgian nationality and the De Greef's handyman.

He was a guide from Anglet and across the border into Spain.

After Dédée was arrested in January 1943 he also accompanied escapers on the trip down from Paris. In March 1943 he too was arrested. The ever resourceful Elvire De Greef (Tante Go) arranged for the local German authorities discover that should M. Jonion be released then details of their illegal black market activities would remain a secret. The next day Johnson was released and quickly spirited over the border.

Once finally back home in Britain Albert worked for MI9 dealing, quite naturally, with the escape lines. At the end of the war he was appointed to lead the Awards Bureau in Paris which was established to recognise the work of European civilians in their war efforts. He was awarded an MBE and died in Tasmania in 1954.

## Ambrosio San Vicente

I have to preface this section with a note that there is so much contradictory and conflicting information about this man that I cannot be sure I have his story all worked out entirely correctly. I have left out what I have been unable to resolve to my own satisfaction, but if anything remains which is not correct then I can only apologise to Ambrosio and his descendants.

He was born in Vitoria-Gasteiz, Spain in December 1902. In 1933 he joined the Araba Buru Batzar (Basque Nationalist Party). During the period of our story he was living at 7 Salagoty Street in Saint-Jean-de-Luz with his companion Marïtxu Anatol. Two evaders from every group that passed down the Comète Line through the area seemed to have spent a day or more sheltered at their home, most left messages in a notebook there.

Ambrosio was also involved with another escape line helping civilians, some French but mostly Jewish, to escape over the border into Spain. The local organiser was an Alejandro Elizalde. It appears that he had a large number of smugglers working for him and they were all probably heavily involved in the black market. This was thought to be a risk by the Comète Line as it inevitably brought them into close contact with the German forces. While the Germans seemed happy enough to turn a blind eye on those activities, mainly because they too profited, assisting evaders and escapers was a different and much more serious matter. But Alejandro's group were in a good position to gather information about the German activities and intentions.

Ambrosio was arrested on the 17th of July 1943. It appears that he was betrayed as a 'Red Basque' by the Spanish police. He passed through several infamous concentration camps including Buchenwald and Flossenbürg. His death is commemorated on the memorial in Flossenbürg, but he was in fact repatriated on the 4th of June 1945 from a different camp in extremely poor health. He died in Saint-Jean-de-Luz in 1971 and is buried there.

**Maritxu Anatol**

She was born in the Basque region of Spain in 1909 and her entire family moved to Béhobie on the French side of the border at the outbreak of the Spanish Civil War. She worked for the local Resistance, the Comète Line and the Margot escape line in obtaining information and provisions and by sheltering evaders. Maritaxu was arrested on the 13th of July

1943 with several of her close group.

She was held by the Gestapo in Bayonne, and later Biaritz. She was extensively, and brutally, questioned in both places but gave nothing away. By her resolute refusal to admit to anything she eventually convinced the Gestapo that she was not involved and she was released.

She died in Irun in 1981

## Françoise Usandizaga née Françoise Romaine Halzuet (Francia or Frantxiska)

She was born in Vera in Spain in 1908 and was the widow of Philippe Usandizaga who had died in August 1939. Her farmhouse, Bidegain Berri, was used by the escape line from early 1942 until the 15th January 1943 when she was arrested there with Dédée and three evading airmen.

Francia was sent to Ravensbrück concentration camp where she died on the 12th of April 45.

## Florentino Goikoetxea

This remarkable Basque smuggler was born in 1889. He made 66 crossings of the Spanish border guiding 227 escapers. He was awarded the King's Medal. The tale of his final crossing is told in Chapter 20. He died in 1980.

## Bernardo Aracama

Bernard was born in Zegama in 1898. He moved to San

Sebastian as a young man and opened a garage there. He was a candidate in the general election in 1936 for the Basque National Party. When the civil war started he served in Bilbao and was in Gernika. After the war was lost he moved over the border to France.

He returned to reopen his garage in May 1941 and was soon involved with the Comète line. He took Dédée to her first meeting with Vyvyan Pedick at the British Consulate in Bilbao after her second trip over the border when the Comète line first came to the attention of MI9. He also serviced and repaired the British Consulate vehicles and ran a taxi service. He sometimes sheltered evaders in his own home. He was arrested in November 1943 and eventually sentenced to exile in Madrid, he returned home to San Sebastian in May 1945 and again reopened his businesses. He died there in 1979.

P02603.002

Some of the members of the Comète Line with the Pyrenees in the background, believed to have been taken in 1946. I do not have enough information to identify all of these brave people, though some of them played their part in our story and are included in this appendix.

# Appendix IV

## The Escape Party

Here again I will deal with all of the evaders that our William met in his escape from Belgium. And I will do so in the same chronological order.

### Sergeant Benjamin F Goldsmith

His is a most interesting tale for several reasons. Firstly it shows the really extraordinary courage of the man to get back into his rear turret to fly dangerous missions over occupied Europe. He no longer had the false comfort of 'it could never happen to me', that bubble was well and truly burst. He now knew the cold, hard reality of war. Secondly it dispels a widely held myth about airmen who had been helped to return to Britain from the continent.

The Resistance and Escape lines in Belgium and France had been assured by the War Office that no airman returned by them to the UK would ever be asked to fly over Europe again. While this was technically true, the impression that there would be no question of them falling into German hands and betraying the brave patriots who had previously helped them was just a little misleading. Should an individual airman express a firm desire to get back to the fight then he could again be sent to an operational squadron. Benjamin may not have been asked to go back to operational flying but he was permitted to do so. He not the only example that I have come across.

He served with 149 Squadron RAF as an Air Gunner in Stirling bombers based at Lakenheath.

His first operation was on the night of the 2nd/3rd of May 1942 in Stirling N6081 OJ-G to drop bombs on the docks area of Nantes. Nothing unusual was reported. The captain was Sergeant Clayton and the crew was the same for the trip on the 6th of June when they were shot down.

On the 6th/7th of May he went to Stuttgart in Stirling N6092 OJ-Q as part of Sergeant Witney's crew, again there were no reportable incidents.

On the next night he went with Sergeant Clayton in Stirling N6079 OJ-F to go mine laying in the Baltic Sea. There were no incidents.

Their next trip for Sergeant Clayton and his crew was on the night of 17/18th of May, again to go Gardening, this time in Stirling W7508 OJ-D. Another quiet trip.

On the night of the 19/20th of May Sergeant Clayton again took W7508, this time on a raid on Mannheim. He reported large fires in the target area.

The next outing was not so quiet. They again flew in W7508 to lay mines in the area around the Frisian Islands. They were attacked by a German night fighter and the rear turret was rendered inoperable. Whether Goldsmith was able to get out of the turret or had to wait until they landed is not mentioned, but it would have been a fairly fraught time for him either way. He had had a lucky escape. The German pilot's intention would have been to eliminate the threat from the rear gunner.

The night of the 30/31st of May was the first 1000 bomber raid to Cologne when William and his crew had a bad time carrying out their part in the raid. Clayton's crew were also there in W7508. They returned without incident.

Clayton and his crew were out in W7508 again on the night of the 1/2nd of June for a raid on Essen. They reported no incidents.

Goldsmith's ninth operational trip was on the 6th of June as the rear gunner in Stirling W7508 OJ-D with his usual crew. They were shot down on the way to attack Essen by a Bf110 flown by Oberleutnant Walter Barte 4/NJG4 at 02:27 over L'Ecluse in Brabant, Belgium. Sergeant Dudley James Poynter, the Mid Upper Gunner, also survived but was immediately captured and became a Prisoner of War. After his repatriation he married Doreen M Drowley in 1948, they had three children, Sergeant Poynter died in 1986.

The other six members of their crew perished in the incident. They were interred locally and later all buried together in Adegem Canadian War Cemetery, Oost-Vlaanderen, Belgium. They were:-

Pilot - Pilot Officer Peter Levinge Clayton aged 20 the son of Charles Levinge Clayton and Esta Edith Clayton née Levin, of Bishops Stortford.

2nd Pilot - Sergeant James Hutchison Mouat 22 Son of James Mollison Mouat and Anna Wilson Mouat née Somers, of Inveraray, Argyllshire, Scotland.

Flight Engineer - Sergeant Michael Joseph Kelleher 21 Son of James and Anne Kelleher, of Portstewart, Co. Londonderry, Northern Ireland.

Navigator - Pilot Officer David Morgan Price Jones Born in 1914 in Builth Wells, the son of John and Mary Jones née Williams.

Wireless Operator - Sergeant Thomas Alfred George 27 Son

of Robert Edward and Julia Gertrude George; husband of Eveline George née Ross, of Cleethorpes, Lincolnshire, England. Their son Thomas R was born in late 1942.

Wireless Operator & Front Gunner - Sergeant John Frederick Gwyther Born on the 6th May 1912 Son of John Edward and 1909 Florence Elizabeth Gwyther née Lowe (usually known as Alice). He married Charlotte Myra Lumley-Holmes, in 1940, they had no children.

Having baled out of the stricken aircraft Goldsmith landed in a cornfield, where he hid his equipment under the hedge. Crawling under some barbed wire he fell into a flooded ditch on the other side. When he came to a farm he knocked on the door and called out "RAF." The farmer quickly pulled him inside and showed his location on a map. Using the phrase book and money from his escape kit, Goldsmith offered to pay for shoes, as he wanted to make his way to Brussels, where he had heard there was an escape route operating,

The farmer then took him to the local gendarmerie where he was given coffee and a bed to rest up before being fed. The farmer returned later to take him to the village of Grèz-Doiceau where he spent the night at the home of a man (possibly called Leblicq) who was with the Belgian Resistance. On 7th of June, he was taken to Wavre where he spent the night in a technical institute, with an English woman married to a Belgian (possibly Daisy and Desire Gain). The whole family spoke English. He forgot their names, but reported that the woman's sister was a Mrs. Lovejoy, who lived on The Broadway in Hendon. He was the first English aviator they saw.

On the 8th of June their daughter Raymonde took him to Brussels by the local tram. From there Desire Gain and another man took him to a boarding school for girls at Bodart. He was the first airman to be sheltered there and stayed for about five days. He was taken to a photographer's house who took the pictures to be used for his ID card. Marguerite Van Lier then accompanied him to the home of Carl Servais the radio operator at 28-30 Stevens Delannoy Street in Laeken where he stayed from 11th to the 23rd of June. This is where he met W. R. Griffiths, and the rest of their journey is recounted in Chapter 19.

Shortly after his return to home shores Sergeant Goldsmith rejoined 149 Squadron and continued to serve as a rear gunner. His first operational trip after his return from Europe was on the 4th of September 1942 when he joined the Greenslade crew. This trip to Bremen in Stirling W7628 OJ-B was largely routine and all went well. The navigator was Pilot Officer F C Jones, the others as listed below.

On the 6th the same crew took Stirling BF311 OJ-G on a raid to Duisberg and reported no opposition.

Goldsmith's next mission was on the night of the 15/16th on a trip to the Bay of Biscay to lay mines in the area just south of La Rochelle again in BF311. They reported no incidents.

They also went gardening on the early morning of the 23rd of September in W7628 OJ-B. They had to jettison the mines and return early as the port outer engine failed, and the port inner would only run on reduced power.

On the evening of the October 2nd 1942 the Stirling bomber R9167, call sign OJ-N took off at 19:30 from RAF Lakenheath to bomb Krefeld in Germany. At around 21:30 they were intercepted by a Messerschmitt Bf110 night fighter over Horst flown by Oberleutnant Hans-Dieter Frank and his radar operator/rear gunner Unteroffizier Erich Gotter. They jettisoned the bombs but it made little difference. They still could not shake off the Bf110 which attacked once more. The Stirling crashed in flames.

One of the airmen, Sergeant Ernest Leslie Moore, lay mortally wounded in the field near the wreckage and died before he could be transported to hospital in Venlo. He had pointed constantly to the ring on his left ring finger, and a local chap managed to get the ring off. This was sent to his parents shortly after the liberation. None of the rest of the crew survived the crash. They are all buried together in Jonkerbos War Cemetery.

The crew of the Short Stirling R9167 OJ-N were:

Pilot - Squadron Leader William Roy Greenslade, DFC AFC Age 25. The son of William Henry and Irene Greenslade of Hanna, Alberta, Canada

Flight Engineer - Sergeant Marshal Kenneth Smith Age 21. Son of Leonard Frederick and Emily Gertrude Smith; husband of Evelyn May Smith, of Cambridge.

Navigator - Flight Sergeant Robert Francis McIntyre R.C.A.F. Age 25 Son of Andrew Nesbit McIntyre and Kathleen Mary McIntyre, of Vancouver, British Columbia, Canada.

Wireless Oerator/Air Gunner - Sergeant Frederick Leonard Hughes Age 21. Son of Frederick and Violet May Hughes, of Shoreditch, London.

Wireless Operator/Air Gunner - Sergeant Ernest Leslie Moore Age 20. Son of Ernest William and Kate Moore, of Leicester.

Air Gunner - Flight Sergeant William Orange, born in Bedlington, Morpeth on the 27th March 1915, the son of Robert Orange and Susan Snape.

Air Gunner - Sergeant Benjamin Frederick Goldsmith Born in 1920 in Edmonton, the son of Leopold Jacob and Margaret Marie Bacon, of Prestwich, Lancashire.

There is now a memorial to the crew in Bedelaarspad near Kronenberg.

## Sergeant Reginald John Collins

He was born on February 8th 1913 in Eumundi, Queensland, Australia. He was the front Gunner/Bomb Aimer in Vickers Wellington Mk 2, W5586 call sign EO-U, from 15 OTU operating from Harwell. Although the crew had not quite completed their training they took part in the 1000 bomber raid on the night of May 30/31st 1942 to Cologne. Although unusual, for a 'maximum effort' push some instructors who had completed operational tours, or some of the more capable crews at an advanced stage in their training at various OTUs would participate on active missions.

There are some conflicting reports as to the details of the night's events, but the weight of evidence suggests that they were shot down by a Bf110 flown by Leutnant Helmut Niklas and his Gunner/Radio Operator Unterofficier Heinz Wenning of 6/NJG1. When Niklas' aircraft was hit by return fire from one of the Wellington's gunners he was severely wounded, but managed to make an emergency landing at Saint-Trond airfield. Niklas would be out of action for the next few months.

The crew all managed to get out of the Wellington which then crashed between Waasmont in Brabant and Lincent in Liège Belgium at just after 03:00 in the morning. Of the other crew members, Warrant Officer John Edward Hatton was picked up the next day in the village of Dormaal, he had a broken ankle, Pilot Officer John Harpur, Flight Sergeant R Hill and Sergeant Frederick Raymond Hindle, were also taken prisoner soon after and all four served out the war as a PoWs.

Collins had landed badly and injured a knee. He did not know exactly where he was and decided to try to reach Liège as he had heard that an escape line had operatives there. He may have thought the Germans would expect him to go directly eastwards and so he headed north until it began to get light and hid for the day.

On the following night he made his way more to the south. He came across a column of German tanks, but managed to avoid being stopped. Again he hid up during the day. A couple of farm workers discovered his hiding place, they then led him to somewhere more secure and returned later with some food. Later in the day an unknown man and the local priest provided him with clothes and boots, some more food and some Belgian Francs. They showed him the way to Liège.

Travelling only at night and hiding during the day, he ended up on the wrong road. Fortunately he met a group of young Belgian men who took him to the local mayor. Again he was given food and pointed in the right direction for Liège. He then met another group of Belgian locals who hid him for a couple of days. One of these local chaps put him on the tram for Liège.

Collins thought it better to get off the tram a few stops short of the town and walk the rest of the way under cover of darkness than risk any chance of discovery as he had no ID papers. On the way he was stopped by two gendarmes. They soon discovered his identity, but they simply shook his hand, wished him good luck and directed him to a farm where he could hide for the day. At the farm he was given food and drink, and had his first shave since leaving Harwell.

While hiding the following day, he was once again discovered by a friendly local. This time he was taken to the farm of a Mme Farcy in Bovenistier just south of Wareamme. Here he was given fresh clothes and stayed for a few days. A teacher by the name of Firmin was lodging there and he took Collins to a café near the University of Namur to meet Robert Declercq who was studying law there. Declercq's parents were living in London at the time.

He was taken by train to Gembloux, either by Declercq or one of his contacts in the Resistance, from there the pair walked to Sombreffe. They managed to hitch a ride in a truck from a local brewery. When they arrived at the farm it was found to be unsafe for him to stay there, so they were driven to Haneffe by another friend. From there they make the short journey back to Bovenistier by bicycle.

This time Collins would be under the care of the Priest Father Georges Moussiaux in Limont for a few days. At least now his risk of being discovered hiding in insecure places would be considerably less, he had been found four times so far, fortunately for him by friends and not the occupying forces.

On about the 15th of June Robert Declercq collected him from the good cleric with Firmin and Victor Farcy who was an active Resistance member at just 16 years old, and they took him by train from Waremme to Brussels. On the train they met Denyse Scheuer who would later hand him on to Madeleine Merjay at Schaerbeek station in Brussels. Merjay, in turn guided him to a Dr Andre at 73 Rue Van Artevelde in Brussel. He stayed there for two days and then moved on to 'a hotel' when Jacques Donny would look after him.

On the 23rd of June Georges d'Oultremont took him to the station for a train to Paris, which is where he met William Griffiths and Benjamin Goldsmith, the rest of their journey is recounted in Chapter 19.

After his return to Britain Sergeant Collins retrained as a Pilot and became an instructor. Collins married Elizabeth Kelly in Wandsworth in 1944 and later returned to Queensland where he died in 2000, they had four children.

**Sergeant Marian Henryk Zawodny**

Born 21 November 1919 in Bydgoszcz Poland. He was in the front gun turret of Wellington Z1333 GR-L from 301 Squadron which took off from Hemswell at 22:07 the 10th of April 1942 on a mission to Essen. Just after midnight the Wellington was picked up by multiple searchlights and held for nine minutes. This was when they came under attack from Hauptmann Werner Streib of the Stab I/NJG 1, who was flying a Bf110 from Venlo airfield.

The pilot Wasilewski and Air Gunner Mucha were both wounded and the aircraft set on fire. The crew all baled out successfully, and the Wellington crashed near Broekkant in the Noord-Brabant region. The entire crew survived. The five other crew members were taken prisoner very promptly, but Zawodny managed to evade capture to take his part in our story.

He found the Dutch people to be very frightened of the occupying forces and while some were willing to bring him food and help him to find hiding places, none would actually take the risk of sheltering him in, or even near, their homes. He was on occasions obliged to grub up potatoes to eat. It took him around 10 days to find some partisans brave and skilled enough to smuggle him into Belgium.

For the next week he was hidden by an unknown family in either Charlerois or the nearby village of Mellet. He was visited by a M. Nitelet who may have taken him to his own home or simply checked his Bona Fides and left him where he was. Either way two weeks later he was at M. Dedidte's farm.

He stayed there for another week, which would be around the latter end of May. He was then taken to Pont-à-Celles where an architect M. Simon Jules Gustave Brigode took him in for a week. This is just a few kilometers north of Charleroi and hence a step closer to Brussels. The local butcher and Resistance member 'M. Andre' who, being satisfied that he was genuine, then took him to a local Priest who sheltered him for a further two weeks.

On about the 10th of June Peggy Van Leir went with him to Brussels where he spent just over a week before Peggy and Georges d'Oultremont (Charlie) took him by train to Paris which is where his and William Griffiths' paths crossed. He left Paris on the 16th of July with Dédée and Elvirie with Evans, Angers and Watson. The rest of their eventful journey over the Spanish border is retold on Chapter 20.

Zawodny continued to serve in Polish Air Force after his

return and trained as a pilot before becoming an instructor. He Joined the RAF when the Polish Air Force was disbanded in the UK and served there until 1956. He married and had three children. He died 1993 in Ontario Canada. .

The rest of the crew were :-

Pilot - Flight Lieutenant Jerzy Wasilewski P/1631 /783511 Born in July 1918 in Chotum - held in PoW camp Stalag Luft 3 Sagan & Belaria. Died in Brisbane 1976.

2nd Pilot- Flying Officer Edmund Burszewski P-/318 - held in Stalag Luft 3 Sagan & Belaria. He died in Los Angeles in 1968.

Navigator - Squadron Leader Kazimierz Franciszek Przykorski P/0743 held in Stalag Luft 3 Sagan & Belaria. He died in Plymouth in 1947.

Wireless Operator/Air Gunner: - Sergeant Stephan Mucha P/792823 Born in July 1920 near Wroclaw. He was training as a Wireless Operator in 1939 when the war started and was evacuated with most of the other students to Romania. He made his way through Syria to France and on to Britain in June 1940. He had been flying operationally since the 1st of July 1941 and was shot down on his 21st mission.

His first five weeks as a PoW were spent in a German hospital due to his wounds. The rest of his time was spent in Stalag Luft 3 Sagan and Belaria. He was returned to Blackpool on the 8th of May 1945. He joined the RAF when he was discharged from the Polish Air Force in 1948. He married and had two daughters spending his retirement in Lincoln. He died in 2004.

Rear Gunner - Sergeant Leon Blach P/792864 Born in April

1921 in Wielun (or Tectins). When Poland was defeated by the Germans in 1939 Blach escaped to France through Romania and then on to Britain when France fell. He was a prisoner in Stalag 4B Muhlberg on the Elbe River in Brandenberg. Researching this chap's fortunes I have to wonder how he ended up in a different camp from his crew mates.

I could understand Mucha being apart from the others after spending a few weeks in hospital, but that was not the case. Nor do I yet know how Blach managed to get back to the UK quite so early. He was returned to Blackpool on the 10th of May 1945. Stalag Luft 3 was liberated in April 1945 by the Russian Army, but most prisoners were retained in the camp until late May or early June for reasons that have never been well understood.

Although the British and American troops were relatively well treated by their Russian liberators during this time, the Polish there were not so lucky. Some already 'liberated' prisoners managed to escape across the lines to British or American forces. Perhaps Leon was one of those.

After the war was over Leon Blach settled in Nottingham where he married and raised a family. He died in 2011.

**Privates William MacFarlane and James (Jimmie) Goldie**

These two were privates from the 7th Battalion, Argyll and Sutherland Highlanders which was part of the 51st (Highland) Infantry Division in June 1940 and was attached to French 10th Army. Their task was to cover the retreat of the British Expeditionary Force to Dunkirk and to prevent the advancing German Army from turning to the south and taking Paris. It was to prove to be a hopeless endeavour.

On the 6th of June they were captured together when the Germans overran their position at Abbeville. They were both held in Stalag IX-C near Bad Sulza and by September 1941 they were in the outlying camp outside Unterbreizbach and forced to work in the nearby salt mines.

On the night of the 20/21st March 1942 they made a bold and well planned escape from their prison. They had amassed a quantity of chocolate, biscuits, tinned sardines plus soap, a large quantity of tea, and some cigarettes both for their own use and for bribes or for bartering. They had made rucksacks from salvaged sacking which carried their supplies, but also covered the large 'KG' (Kriegsgefangener which translates as Prisoner of War) stencilled on the back of their blue prison overalls. They wore these blue work overalls over their battledress.

William had made a crowbar in the workshop where he was labouring and forced the lock from a small gate in the compound perimeter. This gate was only used by the women who worked in the kitchen when they left at around 21:00 when two guards entered the compound and unlocked the gate to let the cooks leave. The sentries stayed inside to feed the prisoners returning from the second shift at 22:45 and they then usually left by the main gate.

One of the guards should have remained at the gate but almost always went into the warm dining room. By leaving after 22:45 on that Saturday night they should have almost two full days before the absence was noticed, even the forced labourers got the Sunday off!

It took them a full six days to reach the railway goods depot at Gerstungen. By only walking at night, skirting round even small villages and taking a circuitous route they managed to avoid detection. They hid in a rail wagon full of salt which was going to Belgium.

Here again their attention to detail served them well. The doors were secured by a thick wire through the hasp which had a soldered seal. They broke the seal and unfastened the wire to get into the wagon. They then opened a large vent, got out of the wagon and replaced the wire, although they could not fix the seal it would have needed close inspection to discover their activities. They then climbed back into the wagon through the open vent.

Although their journey by rail was relatively safe, it was by no means First Class travel. The train would only move for a few hours before being taken off the main line to be left standing for hours at a time, usually in a busy railway siding. The trip to Belgium took a full eight days rather than the two that they had anticipated. Not being able to leave their safe hiding place they soon began to suffer very badly from thirst, to the extent that they could no longer eat the food that they still had.

The train arrived in Hasselt on the 3rd of April and in the early hours of the following morning they finally left their wagon. Walking round the outside of the city they found a small stream and made tea, washed and shaved. They also cleaned their boots. More attention to detail, and again this paid off. They were obliged to walk by day for the next two days as they could find no suitable cover in which to hide. But due to their tidy appearance they managed to continue their journey unhindered. Two days later they arrived in Kessel-Lo. There they asked for water at a house and were sheltered for the night.

Early next morning they were taken by bicycle to Louvain where they were placed in the care of 'a Belgian Patriotic Organisation' probably the Witte Brigade of the Belgian Resistance. They were sheltered by Désiré Castermans. After a few weeks they were passed on to the Comète Line when Vincent Brouckmans took them to Thérèse Grandjean in Liège.

On the 15th of April they were taken to the home of Arthur De Groeve who sheltered them until the 16th of May when he passed them on to Pierre De Praetere. Sometime later Andrée Dumont (Nadine) accompanied them to the home of René Coache, and on the 27th of June they were moved once more to Léon Violette's house in Vincennes where they met up with our William and Reginald Collins.

In evening of the 30th of July the pair were split up, Jimmie Goldie stayed on with the Coaches and William MacFarlane was taken by train to Saint-Jean-de-Luz. The Comète Line guides were Dédée De Jongh and Elvire Morelle, the other three evaders were William Joseph Norfolk, Peter Wright and Joseph Thomas Pack. Norfolk was an Air Gunner who baled out of a Halifax of 76 Squadron when it was shot down near Grez-Doiceau in the early hours of the morning on the 2nd of June. Wright was the 2nd Pilot of the same Halifax; they were not to meet again for several weeks. Pack was the pilot of another Halifax of 35 Squadron which was shot down just after midnight on 9th of June near Molenbeersel.

As usual at Bayonne they were joined by Elvire Degreef and her daughter Janine. There were no incidents and guided by Dédée and Florentino the party crossed into Spain on the 1st of August, and MacFarlane finally arrived in Gourock on the

26th.

Jimmie Goldie followed after his pal on August the 15th. He met Geoffrey Silva, Arthur James Whicher and John Angus McLean at the station in Paris. Silva, an Australian from New South Wales, was the Pilot of a Whitley bomber from No. 24 OTU that was shot down over Ransart, near Charleroi on the 1st of August 1942. Whitcher was the Wireless Operator on the same aircraft and was wounded in the leg as a result of the incident. The pair stayed together throughout their little adventure.

McLean, a Canadian from Prince Edward Island, was the Pilot of a Halifax bomber of 405 Squadron which was brought down when on a mission to bomb the Krupps works in Essen on the night of 8/9th of June. The aircraft was hit by flak over the target and badly damaged. Struggling to get home they were intercepted by two Bf110 night fighters and crashed near Bruchem in the Netherlands. They did manage to shoot down one of the attacking German planes. The rest of their crew were taken prisoner within a few hours.

The party was accompanied to Saint-Jean-de-Luz by Jean Frédéric Wittek and guided by Andrée De Jongh and Flonentino. The rest of the border crossing was much the same as MacFarlane's which is recounted above; but due to his wounded leg Whitcher struggled with the rough terrain over the Pyrenees. For much of the journey he was carried on Goldie's shoulders with McLean assisting the pair. This party arrived in Gourock on the 9th of September. As a result of their determination and resolve both Goldie and MacFarlane were awarded the Distinguished Service Order.

## Flight Sergeant Bernard Evans

Usually known as Bunny he was the rear gunner in a Wellington of 15 OTU operating out of Harwell on the night of 30/31st May 1942. The aircraft was shot down by a Bf110 night-fighter near Mot-sur-Marichienne in Hainault Belgium. The pilot, Dennis John Paul, also survived but was taken prisoner. Stanley Maurice Green, Thomas Leo Lyons and James McCormack were all killed. Evans took cover in the local graveyard and was picked up from there on the same night by members of the Belgian Resistance. They managed to get a note written on cigarette paper smuggled in to the pilot informing him that Evans was safe.

On the 2nd of June Mrs. Rose Baude drove Evans to Charleroi and sheltered him at their family home. The next day he was taken to a Mme Spineaux, still in Charleroi, where he spent the following two and a half weeks. He was moved to Brussels when the German security services stepped up their activities in the Charleroi area.

After a few days spent with Mme Spineaux's cousin Evans went by train to Namur with Robert Poreye where he had his photograph taken ready for his new identity papers. Then Jacques Tiberghien took him to the home of Jules Dubois who was the Mayor of Dhuy. He stayed there for two days before the good Mayor took him to Baron Louis de Jamblinne de Meux where he also met Watson. The pair stayed with the baron until the 20th of June when Dubois drove them to Namur, where they met Robert Nicolas de Bayard and his fiancée Suzanne Laurent. They in turn took the pair by train to Brussels and then on to the Cantine Suédoise, managed by Jean Greindl.

Later Andrée Dumont (Nadine) escorted Evans and Watson

to another safe house and she returned there with Pack on the 1st of July to guide them all to Paris, again by train. They were sheltered at the safe house in Villa St-Maur with Angers and Zawodny, until the 16th of July when the party left with Dédée and Elvire Morelle for Saint-Jean-de-Luz. They were joined on the train at Bayonne by Elvire Degreef (Tante Go) and Bee Johnson. The rest of the tale of their eventful crossing of the border is told in Chapter 20.

## Waclaw Czekalski

He was born on the 8th of July 1918 in Wolkowsk Poland which is now in Belarus.

On the night of the 5/6th of May 1942 he was the co-pilot of Wellington bomber Z8599, call sign SM-R from 305 Squadron operating out of Lindolme. They were intercepted by Oberleutnant Wilhelm Herget of the Stab II./NJG 4, flying a Messerschmitt Bf110 near Sart-Saint-Laurent in Namur, Belgium. One engine was severely damaged. Unable to maintain height the pilot, Stanislaw Krawczyk, ordered the crew to abandon the aircraft. One of crew members did not have a parachute. Krawczyk gave him his own and stayed with the stricken aircraft.

Czekalski landed in the woods near Profondville, which is just west of Charleroi. He hid there until it was dark. He then made his way to a farm. He asked where he was and for some clothes. The farmer gave him both food and some civilian clothes then sent him on to Bioul. Later on he moved to Mettet. In a café there he asked for directions to the French border about 40 Km away to the south. At Philippeville Czekalski spent another night in woods before moving on to

Florennes, where he went to another café.

He cautiously made himself know as an RAF officer and was taken by an unnamed man to his home which was close by. The man's wife could speak English. She provided food and shaving gear for him. He spent the night there. The next day, May the 9th he was introduced to a 'garde-champêtre' a local official whose duties were as a Forest Ranger, Countryside Warden and Game Keeper. The chap loaned him a spare uniform and took him on his motorcycle to a small village near the French border south of Philippeville. There he was reunited with Flying Officer Szkuta who did not, at first, recognise Czekalski in his new uniform.

In the evening Szkuta was moved to Namur where Sergeant Siadecki was already staying. The following morning Czekalski was taken by bicycle to Floreffe where he was picked up by car and also taken to Namur. There the three were extensively questioned to confirm their identities. After four nights they were all taken back to Floreffe to pass the night and moved on, again by car, to Dhuy by Dr. Albert Delforge the following evening to the home of François Feron where they would be staying until the 10th of June.

Jules Dubois, the mayor of Dhuy, then took them to Namur station by bicycle, where they met Albert Petit. He passed them on to Robert Nicolas and his fiancée Suzanne Laurent at the Citax garage on Rue Rogier in Namur. Robert and Suzanne accompanied them to Brussels and handed them over to Jean Greindl in a small café near the Luxembourg train station. The guides then went with him to the Cantine Suédoise.

They then went by train to Leuven from where they were taken care of by Andrée Dumont (Nadine) who took them to

Paris on June 19 or 20th. There, she entrusted them to a man who took them to Frédéric De Jongh (Paul). They were separated. Siadecki went to a small grocery store in Asnières, where they stayed for four days. As there were only four places for each trip to Spain, the members of the network decided that the three British airmen should have priority, although they arrived had later. Sergeant Czekalski accompanied them, while Siadecki would have to wait in Paris for his turn.

The story of our four evaders' trip home is told in Chapter 19. The rest of the crew also had their own adventures in Belgium.

The crew were:-

Pilot Flying Officer Stanislaw Krawczyk P/1347 Krawczyk did manage to make a successful crash landing nearby after which he too managed to evade capture. For this remarkable action he would later be decorated with the Virtuti Military, 5th class. He was killed in action on the 1st of November 1942 flying in Wellington R1716.

Navigator Flying Officer Alojzy Szkuta P/76625

Wireless Operator Pilot Officer Kazimierz Rowicki P/0148

2nd Wireless Operator Sergeant Edward Mikołaj Siadecki P/792851

Air Gunner Sergeant Ludwig Czarnecki P/781566 Sergeant Czarnecki was the only one to be captured; he had broken his leg as a result of the parachute descent. He served out the war in Stalag Luft 3 Sagen and Belaria PoW camp.

After his return to Britain Sergeant Waclaw Czekalski

retrained as a pilot and continued to serve in front line duties. On the 11th of April 1944 he was the pilot of Wellington HF188 of 304 Squadron on anti submarine patrol over the Bay of Biscay when it was shot down by a Ju88 Nightfighter. Sergeant Edward Siadecki was once again his Wireless Operator.

The rest of crew were:-

Co-pilot Flight Lieutenant Lech Kazimierz Małynicz P/0463

Squadron Leader Edward Tytus Stańczuk P/0049 /76889

Flight Sergeant Edward Mikołaj Siadecki P/792851

Flight Sergeant Franciszek Matlak P/781111

Flight Sergeant Bogusław Szpinalski P/703941

There was an extra crewman on the aircraft, Podpulknowik (Wing Commander) Stanislaw Poziomek P/0087 His was the only body recovered and identified. He is buried in Bilbao British Cemetery.

# Epilogue

I hope, in future editions, to be able to add here that:-

William's grave is no longer unmarked.

A memorial has been established at the recently found crash site near Plancenoit.

N R Hartley's fate has been discovered, I do now have some clues to follow up.

www.ingramcontent.com/pod-product-compliance
Ingram Content Group UK Ltd.
Pitfield, Milton Keynes, MK11 3LW, UK
UKHW020749280225
455691UK00012B/520